HIT YOUR BULLSEYE!

JOHN NICHOLAS

Book Interior and E-book Design by Amit Dey
Cover design by Cruzial Designs

For information about this title or for Quantity Sales Discounts, Bulk orders or Special Group pricing contact the publisher:

Nicholas Group Publishing
McKinney, Texas
214-695-8558
Email: hello@hityourbullseye.com

ISBN: 978-1-7361587-2-2 (print)
ISBN: 978-1-7361587-3-9 (eBook)

TABLE OF CONTENTS

DEDICATION

This book is dedicated to the memory of my good friend, Tim Antioch. Tim lived like a blazing meteorite in flight, fueled by his almost boundless enthusiasm for people and for life, which naturally produced his warmth, generosity and humor. Tim could be a bit loud, but he was never too proud to accept correction, to apologize or to laugh at himself before resuming his full-blast assault on life. Tim's journey featured multiple seasons, talents and interests (including his time working in the music industry), but his ultimate destination became clear to him and to everyone he told about the open arms of Jesus, over the years. Tim rocked the world, overcame setbacks, enjoyed some success, loved his family and lived a truly epic and on-target life.

INTRODUCTION

A TRULY EPIC LIFE?

The view from the modern $35 million cliffside mansion overlooking Sydney Australia's Victoria Harbor was glorious, from the iconic Opera House reaching toward the sky to the famous Harbor Bridge arching beautifully over the sparkling waters below.

As I watched one of Sydney's top real estate brokers tour the property on Amazon Prime's *Luxe Real Estate* TV show, I had to agree with his opinion as he surveyed the scene and proclaimed, "This view is epic!"

But I had to cringe when I heard him say the same thing three times within just a few minutes.

It reminded me how overused the word has become these days, when we hear people – and maybe even ourselves – call everything from tasty tacos to spine-tingling experiences, "epic."

It's become a pet peeve of mine, in fact, and has caused me to question whether I should use the word in this book's subtitle, even though it truly belongs.

Since I obviously stuck with the word, let me explain what it means to me and why I hope it will mean the same thing to you.

EPIC IS GREEK TO ME

Like the memorable father in the award-winning 2002 film, *My Big Fat Greek Wedding*, I sometimes like to share the origin of words…going all the way back to their original – and often ancient – Greek meanings.

It comes from my Greek heritage and pride, I think, as the descendent of a Greek immigrant grandfather who landed in Chicago back in the early 1900s where he and his brothers sold flowers and fruit baskets on busy street corners and later built some of America's first shopping centers – allowing him to retire in a stately brick mansion on the last turn of Sheridan Road, overlooking Lake Michigan, in what is now a registered historic home.

The word epic takes us back to the original Greek word, "*epikos*," which means poem or story, usually about gods or heroes, deeds or adventures, usually sung like songs by poets in ancient times – not so different from rappers telling stories today.

Homer's *The Iliad* and *The Odyssey* are the most famous examples.

So, just to be clear, epic means a whole lot more than just awesome or fantastic, no matter how great those ocean views or tasty tacos might be.

It follows then, at least in my book, that an epic life is all about poetry and drama, heroism and bravery, tragedy and victory, destiny and so much more – complete with flying arrows, falling empires, divine interventions and the like.

This is the epic life I'm talking about and it's what we're here to explore and pursue together in this book, like a great quest or adventure.

EPIC STUDY, REFLECTION & ACTION

As I share my story with you, we will reflect upon the lives of high-impact people throughout history. We will study everyone from Bible heroes to hi-tech billionaires, along with plenty of fascinating people in between – including you.

That's right. This book is not just about my story or about famous or historical figures or about concepts and theories to consider or to find "interesting" from a safe, detached or skeptical distance. This book is about you, your story, your dreams, your impact, success and happiness and yes, even your destiny.

So, this isn't a book to scan, browse, read casually or take lightly.

I will share real life-changing experiences and perspectives that you have never heard before and I will ask for your emotional engagement and honest reflection as we dig around your life looking for clues, connecting dots and recognizing both toxic material and treasure, the way I have dug around to navigate my life course and destiny.

The graceful, almost effortless part of this experience will be the dot-connecting insights and "Aha" revelations you discover about yourself, even as I share my story or as we look at others. Those are easy and exhilarating. But they will give way to gut-wrenching reflections about your choices, decisions and possibly about wonderful opportunities now awaiting you with folded arms and scary faces, demanding your most heroic self to arise and meet their challenge.

Then you'll need to take serious action to apply the principles and the passion we explore, and to seek after the freshly discovered (or *rediscovered*) visions and dreams that draw you forward like an electromagnet. Because without some real action and determination, nothing changes. Least of all your life's trajectory.

If this sounds too strenuous, too uncertain or too dangerous for you, then now is your chance to exit with no hard feelings. This journey is joyful, amazing and life-changing, but it's not for the faint of heart.

If you do choose to step forward, however, smiling bravely as you turn each page, intent on launching yourself like a whistling arrow toward your ultimate destiny, then here's to the impact, success and happiness of your truly epic life.

Let's go!

PART I

PERSONAL CONVERGENCE

CHAPTER ONE:

MISSING YOUR MARK

It was Halloween night; I was barely 16 and I was in a high-speed car chase with police.

The cop car's siren was howling and its lights were flashing like fireworks in my rearview mirror, as I drove my mother's Ford Maverick like a bat out of hell.

The chase had started a few blocks back where I caught the attention of a hiding squad car with a short and noisy burst of the Maverick's husky V-8 engine. Then I really stomped on the gas when the cop car lit up and started pulling out to get me.

Now I was racing in the darkness of an otherwise safe and festive suburban neighborhood, as trick-or-treaters and their parents saw the flashing lights and heard the siren and my car roaring their way and were bailing out of the streets before I sped past them and bounced through a dip in the road at a stop-sign intersection, sparks flying, with the cops in hot pursuit.

I continued into another neighborhood, screeching through turns, then spotted a long driveway and a chance to duck (and theoretically hide from) my pursuers behind the adjoining house, so I yanked hard that way.

Jumping the curb and tearing across the front lawn, I misjudged the distance and slammed right into the front corner of the house. BAM!

When the officer approached my door, with the front of my car smashed up against the house and a crowd of spectators now forming behind us, enveloped by the pulsating emergency lights on the street, I rolled down my window and said, "So what seems to be the problem, officer?"

Yes, I was a cocky (and slightly buzzed) kid who could have killed someone.

I was living off-target, missing my mark by a mile.

They threw me in jail that night and I got kicked off my high school football team the next day, along with the two friends who made the mistake of riding with me.

ONE WRONG TURN

If you've ever woken up hoping a terrible situation – whether medical, relational or financial – was just a bad dream, only to discover the nightmare was real, then maybe you understand. I was devastated and groaned as I buried my face in my pillow.

What the heck had I been thinking?

Nothing very smart, obviously. At least no one had gotten hurt.

But the damage was done. I felt stupid, embarrassed and sorry to have wrecked my mother's car and damaged someone's home and to have disappointed everyone else; my family, friends, coaches, teammates and especially the cute cheerleader I had just started dating. She had been waiting for me at the gymnasium where our school had hosted a Halloween dance, with great hopes of keeping us off the streets and out of trouble that night.

Then there was my poor mother who had to bite her tongue and shake her head when she looked at me.

My life was now officially ruined before it started. Where had I gone wrong?

The short answer was a stop sign near the school. Instead of turning right at that little intersection and driving over to our campus, I kept going straight – then punched it like a dragster coming off the starting line for a momentary thrill.

That stop sign was exactly one block away from parking near our gymnasium, which meant I was just a block away from my new girlfriend, the cute cheerleader. I could have quickly parked and walked right in with my two buddies who came with me. My eventual crash happened about six blocks away in a slightly different direction, proving how far even a "slightly different" trajectory can send us astray.

It didn't help, of course, that I had drunk some alcohol with friends that evening to celebrate our team's victory that afternoon, before heading to the dance. The weather had been hot as blazes during the game with Santa Ana winds seriously dehydrating our bodies, which probably hadn't helped my reaction to liquor or my decision-making.

My root problem, however, was much deeper than wrong turns, drinking or dehydration. It's a problem that affects many people today and it might affect you, too.

A SERIOUS LACK OF VISION

A famous old proverb says, "Where there is no vision, the people perish."

Does that mean we die? It certainly can. The ancient Hebrew definition of "perish" means several things including "become unrestrained," "behave wildly" and even "wander aimlessly." But whatever your definition, it's not good to perish!

My problem was a serious lack of vision. I didn't have anything great or noble or compelling drawing me toward an important result or destination to keep me on point, on the right path, out of trouble, fully focused or free from casual distractions or foolish decisions.

Like so many people, I was just reacting day-to-day without a master plan or magnetic target.

This reminds me of the old saying, "If you aim at nothing, you'll hit it every time."

Sure, I had some goals that could or should have kept me on track, even at the age of sixteen. I aspired to play college football, for instance. But I was still easily distracted and quickly swayed from whatever path I thought I was on. I was a little bit wild and unrestrained, too!

Without a clear or compelling vision, I was now doomed to wander aimlessly and probably suffer the consequences of my mistake forever…unless I could find some direction or inspiration – and find it fast.

CHAPTER TWO:

DIGGING FOR YOUR DESTINY

What do you do when you've hit the wall (or a house), hurt others, fallen short, failed miserably, embarrassed your family, been delayed, discouraged, detoured or blown completely off course...or when you just don't like where you're at or how things have turned out and you want to either hide forever or throw in the towel?

Hopefully you take a good look in the mirror.

That's what I did, and I didn't like what I saw. I was a dumb jock who needed a serious attitude adjustment, if not a miracle makeover.

So I started apologizing to everyone I could the next day, thanks to my father's rise-and-shine apology tour that included my mother, the homeowners I crashed into and the police who hauled me into their jail just a handful of hours earlier.

Talk about humbling.

I apologized to those VIPs plus all my family members, coaches, teammates and of course, the cute cheerleader. Would they forgive my stupidity and selfishness...or just write me off as a lost cause?

Time would tell. But I couldn't wait around, I had to start digging for my life.

THE UPSIDE OF CRISIS

A wise friend and former airline pilot once told me that the Chinese symbol for "crisis" includes two very different symbols.

"The first one represents danger," he said, "and the other one represents opportunity. Because crisis offers both."

I didn't know that nugget of wisdom at the age of sixteen, but I *sensed* it, probably by sheer animal instinct.

I certainly grasped the danger of my situation, the idea of being a loser for life and a total disappointment to everyone who ever knew me. I was crystal clear about that depressing path and that very possible end to my story. But I also sensed that a tiny spec of opportunity lurked somewhere under the wreckage.

So I dug deep, desperately searching for some shred of identity or direction, some glimmer of hope or vision. Who was I? Where did I come from? And where did I want to go?

It was dark, lonely and rugged, like mining coal with your bare hands.

How could anyone recover from such a painful and public failure, I wondered? How could my epitaph be anything other than some crazy kid who "crashed and burned" at the age of 16?

Thankfully, my support system didn't abandon or condemn me – although my mother still had to shake her head.

SMALL NUGGETS OF HOPE

My football coach was truly sorry he had to kick me and my buddies off the team, as we were all valuable starters. To make matters worse, he had elevated me to start on the varsity squad as just a 158-pound sophomore the year before, which was a rare honor and a clear signal that he saw something special in me. So, he certainly felt the sting of disappointment.

My father, who had always been a "straight arrow" and had briefly played some football at Northwestern University after serving in WWII, also felt some pain as we watched the final games of the season from a distance, on the outside looking in.

For me there were no team dinners, no practices, no end-of-the-season team banquet, honors or awards and no promise of ever playing again.

Thankfully, our no-nonsense ex-marine corps drill sergeant coach, Ken Russell, didn't slam the door in my face or ban me for life. That door was left slightly ajar.

Meanwhile, teachers, administrators, family members and people in the community all seemed to feel bad for me, even as they probably chuckled and made side bets about my future.

There was nothing anyone could do – or undo – to help my plight or brighten my prospects. For most people it was wait-and-see.

I was master of my own fate. Like every person ever born, I had to seek and pursue my own destiny.

And so, I kept digging for hope, for clues, for keys – and unearthed a few that required a closer look.

There were three key nuggets, in fact, that caught my eye and sparked my imagination…and they now demanded my full attention.

CHAPTER THREE:

BURIED TREASURE

Soul-searching isn't very popular these days and neither is digging for buried treasure.

Both require serious time and attention, which most of us lack due to our many duties, distractions and competing interests – unless we're desperate. Which is why, after my disaster, I was doing both at the same time!

During this desperate process I discovered three areas of life that appeared to be like veins of gold or jewel-encrusted keys. We'll call these treasures:

1. Your history.

2. Your dreams.

3. Your DNA.

Now, these treasures didn't appear to me in these exact terms, all clean, bright and shiny. They were not clear-cut subjects "one, two and three" during this desperate discovery phase. They were still covered in muck and mire. Everything was messy and

I wasn't clear about anything. But at a gut level these themes attracted me. I knew I was on to something.

A NEW PARADIGM

I started looking at my life as if I was peering through a magical lens, with a suddenly new way of seeing things.

I looked at my personal history, including my positive and negative experiences as well as those of my family members and relatives. I found myself reflecting on them for insight and inspiration.

When it came to my dreams, I found that they were hazy, distant and almost disconnected from my everyday life. I could see they were buried deep under my teenage doubts, fears and insecurities and that I would need to assess them and take them more seriously.

My DNA, or basic "wiring," was easier to see, as it included my basic talents, personality traits and a simple inventory of what made me tick, what came naturally and what made me happy. But even so, I would need to review these things further in order to cultivate and coordinate them.

This new and holistic perspective began to dispel the chaos and panic that had overwhelmed me, and it started to renew my spirit at least a little bit.

WHAT HAPPENED NEXT

I reviewed my family history. I looked at our various strengths, weaknesses and special attributes and two things stood out. Number one was brainpower, as my parents and brothers were all smart college graduates or current students at prestigious universities. But I was not following in their footsteps or even on the same path. Could I transform myself from being the "bad student" of the family into a good one?

The second attribute was work ethic, going back to my immigrant Greek grandfather, the one who first hustled on the streets of Chicago. As you might recall from this book's Introduction, he eventually developed some of America's first shopping centers and landed in a mansion on Sheridan Road, overlooking Lake Michigan.

That same work ethic drove my father to work full time while earning a graduate engineering degree for his aerospace career (at night), and my mother who put herself through college with very little moral or financial support from her family, then worked several years as a coast-to-coast flight attendant during the glory years of commercial aviation, when everyone dressed up to travel and every flight was an adventure.

On balance, I came from winners. And I had tasted winning for myself after playing for two undefeated football teams during my first two years of organized football, going a combined 23-0.

Could I harness some of that mojo going forward?

Next came my dreams. This one was tough because my deepest and dearest dream looked ridiculously far-fetched if not impossible at that moment.

I had never said it out loud, but deep down I dreamed of playing pro football.

When I was a little guy growing up the NFL was marketing the sport with dramatic slow-motion film clips set to inspirational music and poetic narration. And I was eating it up, totally enthralled and inspired. I watched every game on TV, wore miniature uniforms and played with neighborhood friends till it got dark.

My family members played sports but none had achieved any real success at the college level, let alone made it to the pros. Secretly, I wanted to break that mold to be the first in our family to play serious college sports – and maybe even beyond. My dream was to play on TV, get paid to play my beloved sport and compete with the world's best athletes.

Unfortunately, I wasn't a great athlete myself.

In fact, I had worn leg braces to bed as a toddler because my legs were knock-kneed and pigeon-toed (and they still weren't exactly normal) and I was always kind of skinny for a football player. I was known as a big hitter with confidence and determination but was never the biggest, fastest or strongest on my teams.

To make matters worse I had just finished my junior season by getting *kicked off the team*. Obviously, that was no way to realize a football-related dream!

Fortunately, I had played well and impressed some people during my shortened junior year season, before getting booted. Unfortunately, I had no honors or accolades to attract college scouts who might offer scholarships or invite me to play at their schools, which had been the only real goal I had at the time.

I had missed the most important window of opportunity for recruiting, which typically follows your junior year season.

This meant I was a Nobody – a Nobody with serious red flags attached to my name should any recruiter or college dare take a closer look. As a result, I would be left behind, completely ignored as the recruiting season came and went.

Could I somehow cultivate, feed and pursue my dream, despite all that reality? Was my dream quest pointless and impossible, if not dead and buried?

Last was my DNA. How was I wired? What came easy? What were my natural strengths, interests and personality traits? What made me happy?

This was easy. I was hot-wired for adventure, which probably came from my other grandfather (this one Irish), a lifelong merchant mariner who traveled the world. I was also feisty by nature, a bit of a badass, which I always linked to my Spartan Greek heritage but could have come just as easily from my Irish blood, or from being the youngest of three brothers.

As for my other natural talents or traits, public speaking always came naturally to me. I liked being up front or on stage and naturally loved to create, communicate and lead. I was happiest on a team, in a group, rallying the team, leading the charge toward victory.

Could I somehow find a way to merge all these separate elements in a way that would lead me forward, out of defeat and despair and toward some noble form of impact, success or happiness?

I was about to find out.

CHAPTER FOUR

GONNA FLY NOW

It was time for serious action, a bold attitude and some higher altitude.

Somehow, I started to believe that I could harness the power of my history, dreams and DNA by directing them toward the same target and let them propel me into a real-life "montage sequence" like the ones you see in movies.

You know the kind, where the protagonist gets busy changing his or her life – like the famous training sequence in Sylvester Stallone's classic film, *Rocky*.

The *Rocky* montage featured various action clips spliced together and unified by an uplifting theme song in search of an epic transformation.

In this case it was Rocky waking up early, running through dark and dreary streets, totally alone, an unknown boxer who's out of shape and without much hope or obvious talent. He's trying to respond to a seemingly impossible opportunity (a fight against the heavyweight champion) as the song's lyrics softly join him.

Trying hard now

It's so hard now

Trying hard now

He drinks raw eggs for breakfast and keeps on training, as the music rises and the clips keep coming…

Oh, he's ready

Gonna make a move, yeah

Oh, he's ready

And makin' moves, yeah

Yeah, yeah

Rocky is running faster now, doing sit-ups and push-ups, hitting the speed bag with greater quickness and skill, his strength and confidence growing as his trainer and brother-in-law watch him work…

Getting strong now

Won't be long now

Getting strong now

Now he's chasing a chicken then punching a side of beef in a frozen meat locker, as part of his unorthodox training!

And finally, he's sprinting through the streets, cheered on by a growing crowd of supporters, then up the Philadelphia Art Museum's expansive front staircase, leaping up the last few steps to reach the top, then dances in place with his arms held high as he turns around to rejoice over the city as the uplifting music swells…

Gonna fly now

Flying high now

Gonna fly, fly!

He's become someone special, ready to do something special.

A NEW TRAJECTORY

Like Rocky, I didn't have much time to make things happen. I was halfway through my junior year of high school, with uncertainty staring me in the face on every front. I had to get hopping – if not flying.

Thankfully, every montage is like every one of our lives. It's unique.

Your situation and outlook might not be as urgent or as desperate as mine was, but as you dig to discover and harness your treasure and pursue your ultimate destiny, you will determine the right pace and zeal you need to proceed. The key for any of us, however, is to take action. Bold and determined action.

My montage was fast-paced, and it looked something like the sequence below, accompanied (if you can imagine it) by the song *Eye of the Tiger* from Stallone's later film *Rocky III*, or by whatever psych-up song you know that gets you going.

MY MONTAGE

My eyes open, I yawn, shake my head and get going…I'm eating toast, cracking eggs into a blender and guzzling my chocolate shake …Paying attention in class, raising a hand, taking notes, working with classmates, getting a test back with a "B" (not bad)… I'm lifting weights with friends, talking with coaches, running stairs with the team for off-season training… I'm on a date with the cute cheerleader enjoying some ice cream... I'm in a Key Club meeting speaking to the group, with "Election Speeches" written on the white board behind me... I'm back home reading, taking notes, writing a report, actually listening to my parents... I'm running up a steep hill overlooking the Pacific Ocean at sunset, alone, exhausted, then in my garage lifting some extra weights by myself... I fall asleep reading a book called *Psycho-Cybernetics*... My eyes open again... A smiling teacher hands me a report marked with an "A"... I'm in the school office reading the news on a radio mic reaching every classroom... I'm visiting senior citizens with fellow Key Club members... I'm with the cute cheerleader again, now posing for a spring formal photo... I'm lifting, running, studying, chugging protein shakes... and finally I'm running wind sprints in the darkness of my high school's dimly lit football field, alone, huffing and puffing, looking up at the stars.

TOO LITTLE TOO LATE?

Today I tell people it's never too early or too late to dig, to discover and to harness the power of your personal history, dreams and DNA, and to live on-target.

But as I turned 17 to start my senior year, there were plenty of doubts still crouching outside my door, waiting to assault me.

Real change is never easy, especially when there are well-established doubts in the air, in the people around you or in your own subconscious mind. Old thoughts and habits, other people's judgments and basic inertia are tough to beat, while real transformation often takes a miracle.

But transformation can be simple, too, requiring only a sincere decision, some stubborn faith and a compelling vision to draw you forward.

I was determined to fight through the doubts to reach what I saw in the distance (a vision I cultivated after reading the book noted in my montage above), but no one knew the future or could see what I could see. My vision was still private; I hadn't told a soul. It was too far-fetched. But I had worked hard to alter my trajectory, which everyone could see. Now where would it take me? How far could I turn things around? Did I get started too late?

Only time would tell. But it was time for take-off.

CHAPTER FIVE:

LIKE NUCLEAR FUSION

The two most powerful forces in the universe are nuclear fission and nuclear fusion.

Nuclear fission, which involves the splitting of atoms, is better known to most of us thanks to our familiarity with atomic bombs and nuclear power plants. But experts say nuclear *fusion* creates even more energy than fission, from atoms slamming into each other and merging to form heavier atoms and super intense energy and heat.

As a teenager with little scientific knowledge or interest, I didn't know anything about nuclear fusion. I had never heard of it. But I was experiencing something like it in my life and instinctively understood its dynamics.

Somehow, I understood that by merging key elements of my history, dreams and DNA and directing them toward the same goals or target, I might create some powerful results. And as long as those elements were consistent or in harmony or aligned with each other, anything was possible.

Now, just a little over a year after my Halloween night car crash, these dynamics had merged and taken me to new heights.

HI-RISE RECRUITING

A private invitation-only post-season luncheon was being held on the top floor of the Crocker Bank building in downtown Los Angeles and I was struggling to get there, thanks to my crutches and leg cast.

I had injured my knee in the final game of my senior football season, a playoff game loss to one of Southern California's powerhouse teams. But I couldn't complain. It had been a good season full of exciting team victories and personal achievements, and my knee was supposed to recover without surgery.

Before the season, my teammates had elected me captain after I was reinstated for good behavior, which included my obsessive drive to train and compete and to exhort my teammates to match my intensity. This was an honor I would cherish forever, given their support and confidence in me through all my negative circumstances. It was also a once-in-a-lifetime opportunity (along with being voted Key Club president around the same time) to exercise my leadership gifts and to grow in that capacity.

After the season, I was voted "All-League" on both offense and defense and was also named a *Los Angeles Times* All-Star, a mind-boggling achievement that made me, my family and our team proud.

These accolades followed my breakout season, scoring touchdowns as a tight end and making big hits and highlight tackles all over the field as a linebacker.

But on this day, instead of wearing a grass-stained football jersey I was decked out in a sports coat and tie, riding an elevator to the executive penthouse dining room for a special event honoring LA's top scholar-athletes, hosted by Harvard University as part of their recruiting process.

Thanks to my success on the field and my dramatic improvement in the class-room, I was being recruited by Harvard and by Brown University, that year's Ivy League football champion, plus a number of other colleges. So my confidence was sky-high.

As I sat listening to the speaker, a 6'6" Harvard grad named Pat McInally who played wide receiver and punter for the Cincinnati Bengals and had famously aced the Wonderlic aptitude test given to prospective draft picks, I was surrounded by the region's best and brightest athletes. This included a quiet little guy next to me named Darrin Nelson, who would play for Bill Walsh at Stanford, then 10 years in the NFL.

I was eating great food, listening to a great speaker and enjoying spectacular views of the Hollywood Hills through the room's floor-to-ceiling windows. I had to shake my head and marvel.

PANORAMIC PERSPECTIVE

I had risen from the outhouse to the penthouse in one short year. How did it happen? Was it a fluke? And what did I think about it?

The one thing I knew was the power of a panoramic perspective, whether from a tall building or a place of personal reflection.

Panoramic perspective is our ability to see the big picture from high above, in a holistic or comprehensive way. And with a longer view that helps us focus on our destination more than on the frequently unclear, confusing or overwhelming steps and directions to get there – or on the *distractions* that often keep us from seeing our desired destinations altogether.

I'm basically talking about vision again.

As we will discuss in an upcoming chapter, my favorite definition for vision came from Walt Disney, who said, "Vision is our ability to see the future with imagination." I know you will find that discussion to be worth its weight in gold, but this aspect of vision – a panoramic perspective – is also very important.

Can we see the forest from the trees?

Sadly, we all live in a jungle called everyday life, so most of us need some help climbing higher to see things more broadly. Especially in our own lives.

CONVERGENCE ON DISPLAY

What I saw from my newfound vantage point was something I started calling Personal Convergence, just a few years later.

I didn't know what to call it then, at 17.

But there it was, unfolding before me in the reflection of the office tower's plate-glass windows. My life was unfolding and revealing a mystical if not magical power to chart a course and harness multiple elements of my life to willfully – and to some extent blindly – aim them in the same direction.

Life coaches and self-help gurus have talked about "alignment," and this was certainly similar. The same thing applies to the buzzword of that age, "Synergy," which similar, but was more about cooperating than converging.

Convergence is more powerful, more like nuclear fusion. Here are two definitions of the word from Webster's Dictionary:

1. : the act of converging and especially moving toward union, unity or uniformity // the convergence of three rivers.

2. : the state or property of being convergent (which means "tending to move toward one point or to approach each other").

Even without knowing this word or its definition at that time, I knew I would keep its power in mind as I pressed toward my still unspoken aspirations.

I could only hope – and aim to believe – that my history, dreams and DNA could merge like three rivers into one. One raging river.

CHAPTER SIX:

KERMIT, CORKY, KENNEDY & THE BOYS

As your life converges and flows like a river – or flies like an arrow, sparrow or rocket – you never know who you'll meet along the way, or how they will affect your journey.

I believe it depends on your vision, direction and ultimate destination.

But I know for a fact that if I stayed on my "dumb jock" path to nowhere, I never would have met or befriended the fellow travelers who helped me in totally unforeseen and unimaginable ways.

I simply never would have met them.

MY BIG WORKOUT BUDDY

The biggest dude I had ever seen was about to cross my path – literally. I was walking home from my high school gym (with my leg cast off and my knee recovery now in full swing) and was passing by our school's track, where this huge guy had just finished running laps.

As I walked his way, I realized he must be the Los Angeles Lakers basketball player people were saying had bought a house near our school. He smiled as I approached and seemed friendly, so I slowed down to meet him.

"Hey, I'm Kermit Washington," he said, "what's your name?"

I told him my name and he brightened and said, "Hey, I've heard about you!"

"You have?" I said, both flattered and perplexed.

"Yeah, I've been asking around to see if anyone trains hard around here," he answered. "So I've heard about you."

Now I was speechless, and probably blushing.

"I've got a gym at my house and you're welcome to come lift with me any afternoon," he said, and then told me where his house was.

"I'm serious," he said, reading the disbelief on my face. "I've got a full Olympic weight set up, dumbbells, cables, the whole works."

He didn't have to ask twice. I thanked him and promised to swing by soon.

As we parted ways he turned back with another smile and with a chuckle to assure me, "Just come ready to work!"

Obviously, I thought to myself, shaking my head.

Kermit Washington was a 6'8" power forward in the NBA with a football player's physique and a personal gym to match, when most basketball players still believed weight training would mess up their shooting touch.

What I quickly learned about Kermit, after meeting his friendly wife and adorable daughter, was that he understood his shooting skills were limited, so his success depended 100% on hustle, toughness and hard work.

He knew his role was doing the dirty work for his team underneath the basket, boxing out, rebounding, banging bodies, making a few easy shots and contesting everything. Being physical.

So I started joining him several days a week and we worked hard, lifting weights and counting reps until our muscles screamed and we got dizzy or almost passed out. It was a pro football player's workout, if not a Gold's Gym bodybuilder's workout.

Kermit was hitting the iron like an NFL pass-rusher, not an NBA sharp-shooter.

Kermit's mentality, like his easy laugh, lack of foul language and sometimes grandmotherly comments like, "Oh my goodness!" were funny and infectious. His mental approach was also contagious and perfect for me, given my somewhat limited size and talent.

My only prayer for success at the college level – like his at the pro level – was going to be desire, toughness and hard work. That had been his ticket to a pro basketball career, and I was eager to make it my ticket to something similar as I prepared for college football.

We trained together that spring and summer, sometimes with fellow Lakers dropping by to watch the heavy lifting and sometimes with a few of my friends joining us to work out. I assumed we would keep working out together for years – until Kermit got into serious trouble.

During a game against the Houston Rockets later that year, when I was back East at college, Kermit got into a scuffle with their players while trying to protect his teammate, Kareem Abdul Jabbar. Tragically, Kermit instinctively swung at an opponent rushing in from his blindside and it quickly (and infamously) became known as "The Punch" that almost killed Houston Rockets All-Star forward Rudy Tomjanovich.

Kermit was devastated and was soon traded away from the Lakers, first to Boston then to San Diego and then to Portland, forcing him to move away from the Los Angeles area. I was able to visit him and his family once in Portland, but staying in touch became more difficult as the years passed.

Kermit Washington's example and friendship would last forever in my heart, however, while his work ethic had become my own.

He had sparked much greater faith in my dreams, as well, just by osmosis. I learned that a pro athlete's confidence, like a great work ethic, is contagious and I caught both by spending time with him.

MY KILLER JOB & SECRET FRIEND

Good jobs are hard to find between high school and college.

This is especially true when your only experience is umpiring Little League baseball games, and when you will have to leave town early before summer ends to report for your college football camp.

Thankfully, a super nice friend named Tracy Kennedy got me a job at Marineland of the Pacific, just down the coast from where we lived. It was home to the world-famous killer whales, Orky and Corky.

Thanks to my leadership experience, Tracy was able to pitch me into a job that skipped the usual entry-level ticket-taking, food-vending, trinket-selling or clean-up positions given to new employees.

Tracy got me hired onto her elite squad of ushers who worked a revolving schedule of sea lion, dolphin, pilot whale and killer whale shows, with lots of free time in between to read, relax or just stare at the ocean from Marineland's clifftop location.

Our job was simple. We were there to welcome and direct the guests, answer questions and make announcements – usually asking people to squeeze tighter so we could fit more folks into the stadium bleachers. This was perfect for me as an extrovert public speaker who loved addressing the crowd, "Ladies and gentlemen, can I have your attention please!"

During that summer, numerous sea lion and pilot whale shows got canceled due to illness, creating scheduling gaps that gave us even more free time – sometimes enough for me to literally drive home to run, lift with Kermit or go swimming with my girlfriend (yes, the cute cheerleader), then rush back to work – all while on the clock!

Other times I'd stay to read or play with Corky the killer whale.

Corky was the female star of the daily killer whale shows featuring her and Orky, her big mate. She would frequently interrupt their scripted performances by splashing the crowd or stalling underneath trainers, slowly submerging beneath them for fun.

She was probably bored with their limited space and lack of spontaneity, so she provided some of her own – until Orky got tired of waiting and slammed his pectoral fin against the water with a loud, BOOM! He was all business. He wanted to perform his high jumps and breaches, eat his rewards and finish the shows.

In between shows I would play tag with Corky when no one was around.

I would get her attention, then move around her four-story-tall tank, quickly hustling up and down the different levels to tap on various windows, where she would come and find me, then we'd meet up top where I would slap the tank edge where we could share more face time, eye-to-eye.

Marineland would eventually close and sell its land to developers and Orky and Corky were shipped off to Sea World. But Corky and I would be friends for life, as far as I was concerned. And our connection reminds me how amazing (and surprising) our life journeys can be.

MY FORKLIFT ALL-AMERICANS

The following summer a neighbor got me a job at LAX, working in the Continental Airlines freight warehouse, earning twice what my friends were making in their summer jobs. Such were the perks of being a college athlete.

The only problem was this job was on the graveyard shift. And after working there for a couple months, during the tomb-quiet jet-fuel-scented overnight hours, I started believing that some of the long-term, long-exposed workers had turned into zombies!

There was plenty of life there that summer, however, namely my fellow short-term co-workers Billy Don Jackson and Freeman McNiel, two football stars from UCLA. I had played against Freeman in a post-high-school all-star game and knew Billy Don by reputation as a top national recruit and freakish athlete who singlehandedly saved his family from a fire back home in Texas, as legend had it.

Billy Don was loud, funny and never stopped talking as we raced our forklifts around the warehouse, talking trash and occasionally moving objects as needed. Meanwhile Freeman rarely said a word but also seemed to enjoy the speed of our heavy machinery, and only grudgingly acknowledged that my all-star team had beaten his. He seemed to be biding his time, with his sights set hard on a better destination.

Billy Don Jackson eventually got into trouble, got distracted and never realized his potential. Meanwhile, Freeman stayed focused, worked hard and later became the New York Jets' all-time leading rusher over an illustrious 12-year career.

Their brief friendship, or at least their comradery, provided another unexpected boost to my confidence. These bigtime athletes were on my flight path and they seemed to confirm that I was heading somewhere special.

MY CLASSMATE, THE CROWN PRINCE

John F. Kennedy Jr. was the most famous young man in the world back when I was growing up and was later voted *People Magazine's* "Sexiest Man Alive."

John's life had been lived out on magazine covers with iconic photos showing him playing with his father in the White House and bravely saluting his father's casket after his assassination, followed by others with his sister and their glamorous mother Jackie-O and his world-famous stepfather Aristotle Onassis, the Greek shipping tycoon.

John was the crown prince of American politics and probably would have broken the internet with Likes and followers if they had existed at the time.

John shocked the world when he chose to attend Brown University in 1979 instead of his father's alma mater, Harvard. But that was part of his charm, seeking his own path, knowing his own mind. Brown was also the Ivy League's hottest spot at the time with its less restrictive curriculum, one which fostered freedom and exploration, so he was there on his own quest.

John Kennedy surprised me one day soon after he arrived on campus, when he walked into a small classroom in an old brick building with squeaky wood floors and sat right next to me, with a casual nod and a friendly "Hey" to me and a dozen other classmates.

He didn't really belong in that (upper level) Political Science course as a freshman, but there he was.

I have written elsewhere about the incredible halo effect that surrounded John, with his profound mixture of confidence and humility, all wrapped into one smart, handsome and easy-going package. But it really was something.

We were there to study the Vietnam War with lots of reading and discussion of the controversial *Pentagon Papers,* which revealed heart-breaking truths and long-buried secrets about the war, along with the Pulitzer-Prize winning book *The Best and the Brightest* about President Kennedy's leadership team that wrestled with how to oppose communism without embroiling America in a costly and unwinnable war.

Sometimes these discussions pitted John and me against each other, with me the West Coast conservative and him the East Coast liberal, but usually the facts and common sense led us to common ground and shared perspectives. We became friends in the process and learned a whole lot about life, history and politics.

We talked even more about sports. John loved to discuss pro and college football games with me and our professor after each weekend, including a review of my performance on our school's team, and his own growing interest in rugby, which he would play on the University's club team.

I will always remember how John approached me one day, a year or so after that class ended. It was after I had signed a pro football contract and was about to leave campus and skip graduation ceremonies to attend pre-season football camp. So, it was an emotional time for me.

I was eating alone in the cafeteria one afternoon when John sat down and joined me like a long-lost friend. He was full of curious questions and great enthusiasm about me and my future, about my next steps and great hopes for the future.

He expressed more sincere interest and support during that one conversation than anyone else had before, whether on campus or elsewhere. Because he was so comfortable and secure in his own skin, he could genuinely celebrate my success and my aspirations, without suffering from personal comparisons, insecurity or jealousy.

His friendly interest in me and toward all of life's adventures left a lasting imprint on my soul. It also produced a confidence in me to relate with people from any background, no matter how high or low, and gave me a joyful spirit to pursue all life has to offer.

PATHS, PEOPLE & POSSIBILITIES

Do I share these stories to brag or to impress you?

Yes and no. These friends came to me freely and effortlessly as gifts, so I have nothing to brag about. But I do want to impress you.

I want to impress you with hopeful expectations for amazing discoveries, divine appointments and special people on your own one-of-a-kind flight path or riverbank.

I share my stories to provide memorable examples of what can lie ahead for you and to offer you questions and takeaways for your journey.

Did you notice how these friendships happened organically due to the path I chose to pursue? Kermit never would have recognized my name or invited me to train with him if I had stayed off course without vision or direction. My reputation would not have come to his attention. He never would have heard of me.

If I hadn't changed my outlook and trajectory, hit the books, sought leadership positions and devoted myself to my sport I never would have gotten the Marineland job, played tag with Corky, raced forklifts with Freeman and Billy Don or talked history and sports with JFK Jr. I never would have been anywhere near them!

I never would have gained these relationships or the confidence and wonder that came with them if I didn't change my life course and trajectory.

So, what about you? Can you imagine how your dream or vision-inspired life can lead you toward incredible new people, opportunities and possibilities?

Do you think it's fair to anticipate or even to *expect* that amazing new people and possibilities will meet, greet and encourage you as you aim and commit yourself toward your dream, goal or ultimate destiny?

These questions lead us to the importance of "acting in faith" and to another friend of mine who rewrote history while demonstrating the power of personal convergence – right in front of my eyes.

CHAPTER SEVEN:

THE AMAZING STORY OF BRAD BLANK

My dorm room phone was disconnected, and I couldn't afford to pay the bill.

Too many expensive long-distance calls to my girlfriend on the West Coast, the cute cheerleader 3,000 miles away.

It was now the spring semester of my senior year at Brown University and quite possibly the biggest day of my life. And I needed a phone.

The NFL draft had come and gone without my name being called by any team. That wasn't a big surprise, despite my senior season stat line boasting 11 quarterback sacks, 118 tackles and an interception. I was a 6'1" 225-pound linebacker with pretty good speed, strength and "pop," but was still just a small college player.

I wasn't any NFL team's pick of the litter.

But now came the all-important period when NFL teams could call to offer you a contract as an undrafted free agent if you were an intriguing prospect – and if you had a phone!

The best I could do under the circumstances (with cell phones still a distant twinkle in the future) was to give a friend's phone number to our athletic department in case they heard from any teams trying to contact me.

That whole scenario was a long shot, but I had just enough faith to give it a shot.

Since my phone was disconnected, I gave them the number of my good friend and fraternity brother across the hall, Brad Blank.

A DIFFERENT KIND OF ANIMAL HOUSE

Even a progressive Ivy League college like Brown University had one or two alpha-male jock fraternities back in my day, with behavior reminiscent of the classic John Belushi film *Animal House*. But our house wasn't one of them.

My fraternity was comprised of an interesting mix of guys, including whip smart intellectuals, sarcastic stoners and a dozen or so jocks including star quarterback Mark Whipple. Mark helped recruit me and my closest buddies to the house, then graduated to become a Super Bowl winning coach with the Pittsburgh Steelers and a national Division I-AA champion head coach at UMass, among other highlights.

We also had funny dudes like Ian Maxtone-Graham, who became a writer for *Saturday Night Live* along with iconic characters like Tom Meyers, a lanky engineering student known by his self-given nickname "Grinder," whose signature look included long hair and thick glasses. Tom had been my freshman dorm roommate and had come along as part of a package deal with me and a few of my football buddies who knew him. Tom would later do bionic eye research at Stanford University.

Then there was my good friend Brad Blank across the hall.

Brad was small in stature but he was a huge sports fan and a good friend of many athletes, including some pros he had met at charitable functions over the years. He was also a savvy pre-law student and entrepreneur from a politically active family with close ties to the Kennedy and Shriver clans of Hyannis Port, Massachusetts.

In fact, Brad had invited me to stay with his family in Hyannis Port for a few days before reporting to football camp that summer and had taken me water skiing with Maria Shriver and one of her brothers, alongside the famous Kennedy compound. As a Southern California surfer and political science major I thought that was pretty cool.

A STAR IS BORN

I didn't hear Brad's phone ring across the hall, but I heard him hustle over to knock on my door.

"Hey, John!" he yelled. "Some team is on my phone for you."

I opened my door and hustled over to his room to pick up his phone. On the other end was a pro football team general manager and his team's head coach on a speaker phone.

They said they had heard great reports about me from NFL scouts and wanted to offer me a contract to come play for the Calgary Stampeders of the Canadian Football League, otherwise known as the CFL.

Unfortunately, they were unknown to me. I was only vaguely aware of the CFL.

My thoughts and questions were swirling as they offered me a signing bonus and a good salary if I made the team. They needed a new middle linebacker and they liked my chances to fill that role. So, did I want to sign with them?

That's when I looked at Brad and said, "Can you talk with these guys?"

Brad nodded yes, so I gave him the phone. A few minutes later Brad hung up, told me he had sweetened their deal by a few thousand dollars and that they'd be waiting for my decision.

Did I want to take their offer or wait to see if any NFL teams would call with a better offer? That was one question.

The bigger question for our purposes here is why I asked Brad to represent me in the first place, when I was fully capable of representing myself?

The short answer is that personal convergence was now happening in Brad Blank's life, and I was able to recognize it.

The day before he had negotiated two other free agent contracts for our fellow fraternity brothers, Rick Villella and Steve Curtin, with the New England Patriots and Oakland Raiders respectively. So it was only natural for me to put Brad on the phone to represent me as well – even though he was just my little-brother-sized buddy in his junior year of college!

I knew there were some hidden dynamics at play in his life, as well.

Just as my friendship with Kermit Washington had boosted my confidence (and trajectory) toward pro sports, Brad's secret vision to become a sports agent was bolstered by his friendship with the Godfather of the sports agency business, Bob Wolff, the agent for Boston Celtics superstar Larry Bird and other top athletes of that day.

I knew Brad had formed some kind of relationship with Wolff through his family or friends around Cape Cod and that bolstered my confidence in him. All his interests, dreams and aptitudes were converging as he negotiated for me on the phone.

MAKING HEADLINES AND HISTORY

The press conference was held downstairs in our Theta Delta Chi living room a couple days later, with Brad, Steve, Rick and I taking questions from newspaper reporters and posing for pictures to commemorate the event.

Brad Blank had just become the youngest agent in pro football history.

He had successfully negotiated three pro contracts when he was several years younger than super-agent Leigh Steinberg had been when he represented his friend and first client, quarterback Steve Bartkowski, as a law school student at Cal-Berkeley, a few years earlier. Thus Brad was now the youngest ever.

As Brad's story was shared on various news platforms, all three team general managers were quoted as saying Brad's professionalism was on par with other top agents and that they assumed he was a 30-something lawyer in a nice suit and shiny office, not some kid wearing jeans and a T-shirt in a messy frat house!

Brad's personal history, dreams and DNA had converged to provide a historic opportunity.

Opportunity had knocked but someone had to open the door.

Brad had to seize his opportunity. He could have frozen, lost his nerve, handed the phone back and passed on the opportunity. But he didn't shrink back or let it pass when it arrived unannounced and unexpected when the pressure was high and the chips were down. That's a lot harder than it sounds.

It reminds me of Eminem's famous song *Lose Yourself*, from the film *Eight Mile*:

> *If you had one shot, or one opportunity*
> *To seize everything you ever wanted in one moment*
> *Would you capture it or just let it slip?*

Brad had to act in faith that he was the right person at the right time and place. And Rick, Steve and I had to believe (have faith!) that he was the right person to take the phone and handle our business rather than handle it ourselves.

The next year Brad experienced a rocket boost to his career when he represented a Yale linebacker and former All-Star game teammate of mine from Southern California named Jeff Rohrer, when he was drafted in the second round by the Dallas Cowboys.

The rest is history as Brad became one of the most prolific NFL agents of all time, representing top picks and bigtime players like D'Brickashaw Ferguson, Tedy Bruschi, Chris Canty, Marcellus Wiley and even Tom Brady, on a few marketing deals.

Brad would ultimately negotiate four contracts for me with teams in the CFL, NFL and USFL, and he remains a lifelong friend today.

He also remains the first eye-opening example of personal convergence I observed outside of my own experience, up close and personal.

I couldn't wait to see what would happen next and wondered what more I could learn about the amazing dynamics I had witnessed.

His success also launched me toward the stars – or at least somewhere in that direction!

CHAPTER EIGHT:

YOUR COLLEGE EXAM

I had to take my college exams before I could explore the universe beyond the first chapters of my life.

Now it's your turn.

Whether you've gone to college or not, whether you like taking tests or not, or have no idea what chapter of life you're in right now, this exam (or pop quiz, as the case may be) is mandatory for you at this point in this book. Okay, maybe not mandatory but I hope you'll play along.

It's time to check your comprehension of what you've read so far and learn what conclusions you've reached about our journey, just to make sure we're on the same page. And maybe to have a little fun while we're at it.

Below are several multiple-choice questions, plus an essay question you can answer or at least ponder, along with an answer key you can check to see how well you know your stuff. So here we go...

1. **The basic goal of this book is to help you:**

    A. Improve your archery skills

    B. Learn how to throw darts (or axes) at your local bar or pub

    C. Miss your mark and fall short of your full potential

    D. Experience an epic life of impact, success and happiness

2. **Some common reasons we miss our mark are:**

    A. We take the wrong turns and make bad decisions

    B. We become aimless due to a lack of vision

    C. We get distracted or overwhelmed by everyday life

    D. All the above

3. **The treasure we can study to direct our path is:**

    A. Whatever we can find with a metal detector

    B. Key elements of our personal history, dreams and DNA

    C. Any watches, rings or jewelry that we have

    D. Any diamonds rated "eye clean" or better

4. **Rocky's training montage (or mine) was used to:**

    A. Dramatically illustrate how vision can inspire action

    B. Prepare you for a heavyweight boxing match

    C. Encourage you to consume raw eggs

    D. Show the benefits of running up hills and stairs

5. **The value of panoramic perspective is:**

    A. To gain a healthy big-picture view of things

    B. To see your destination, not just your obstacles

Your College Exam 47

C. To observe how various parts of your life converge

D. All the above

6. Personal convergence is:

A. Some kind of weird New Age concept

B. Similar to nuclear fusion

C. When multiple aspects of your life powerfully merge

D. Both B & C

7. The stories about Kermit, Corky, Kennedy & The Boys illustrate:

A. Why we should never talk to strangers

B. How life-changing encounters don't ever happen

C. How you can never expect help from anyone

D. How you can expect amazing people and other wonders on your path

8. Essay Question: How has my story or the topics we've covered so far resonated with you and your life?

Take a moment to write down your answer, jot down some notes or just reflect in your own mind. And feel free to share your thoughts with me at essays@HitYourBullseye.com.

ANSWER KEY

1. D – Of course! That's where we're aiming.

2. D – Yup, those are our obstacles.

3. B – Hopefully that much is clear so far.

4. A – Yes, clear vision and dramatic action are usually required.

5. D – This perspective is one of our main takeaways.

6. D – It is a powerful force indeed.

7. D – Yes. Keep your eyes open!

8. Go to <u>essays@hityourbullseye.com</u> if you'd like to share.

Now let's turn the page and see where our journey takes us next...

CHAPTER NINE:

CHASING YOUR DREAM

C hasing dreams can be costly, risky and really quite lonely. That's what I was thinking as I looked out the window on my long flight to Calgary, Canada, totally alone and feeling like I was headed to Mars.

I was skipping my college graduation ceremonies to attend CFL pre-season football camp, which starts a couple months earlier than NFL camps.

This meant I was forsaking an epic 2-day graduation weekend (yes, I said epic) featuring a full schedule of dinners and dances, music concerts, sporting events, family activities, speeches and the symbolic march of graduating students along with older – sometimes ancient – alumni through the historic Van Wickle gates at the front of the college, founded all the way back in 1764. Surrounded by family members and friends wishing you good luck and Godspeed toward your future.

It also meant I was flying north instead of due west into the arms of my brand-new fiancé, the cute cheerleader who got my call and marriage proposal over the phone as soon as I signed my pro football contract, cashed my signing bonus and paid my phone bill.

Our wedding would have to wait until after the season, of course – if I could make the team.

If I could earn a roster spot on the Calgary Stampeders I would return home as a victorious hero with some money in my pocket, ready for a fantastic wedding and honeymoon. If I didn't make the team, I would return home emptyhanded, with a cloud of uncertainty over my head and without much fanfare to start my post-college life, already behind my contemporaries in their much safer jobs.

I was excited by this challenge and the adventure ahead yet scared to death by the obvious risk – like a novice mountain climber heading toward an assault on Mt. Everest. In my case there would be no ropes, pitons or safety nets.

There was no easy way to make a professional football team manned by grown men fighting to keep their positions and feed their families. Those were the veterans who knew the coaches, the system, their teammates and all the tricks of the trade to make you look bad and send you home heartbroken.

Then there would be a couple dozen rookies signed from colleges all over the place, along with older free agents with previous pro football experience playing for other teams – all former college stars in their own right – scratching and clawing to scale the mountain ahead of you to win one of the two or three open positions on the team each year.

Their goal was to see you get cut from the team and sent home ASAP.

BLIND AMBITION & SUPREME CONFIDENCE

The only way to enter such intense competition and overcome such fearsome odds is to meet it with blind ambition and supreme confidence.

The Oxford Dictionary defines ambition as *"the strong desire to do or to achieve something, typically requiring determination and hard work."*

By this point in my journey, ambition was hard baked into my personal history, dreams and DNA, and confidence had formed like icing on the cake.

In fact, my confidence on the field had become outright swagger, thanks probably to an interception I returned for a touchdown to win a game against Cornell during my sophomore season at Brown. That highlight had been followed by a variety of other big plays including the eleven quarterback sacks I logged my senior year.

I had become such a flashy player I was nicknamed "Hollywood" by one of my college teammates. I played with passion and with fire and even talked a little trash to my opponents, back before that was such a common thing.

My point here again is not to brag about myself but to point out the importance of building your confidence as you develop skills and hone your talent through successful repetitions, confirmations and memorable achievements.

The bigger your dream or more competitive your field of endeavor, the greater your ambition and confidence must be. Otherwise, the cost, risk and loneliness will eat you up and spit you out.

We will look carefully at how to assess the costs and risks of chasing your dreams in a later chapter. We will also talk further about the sometimes lonely process of pursuing your unique dreams and destiny. Even with family or community support it's still usually a solo act.

In my case, I had two chips on my shoulder to help fuel my fire.

One was being snubbed by major college recruiters because of my size, coming out of high school. I weighed barely 200 pounds at that point, mostly because I was young for my grade level and still growing. So, I arrived on the small college stage determined to bulk up and "ball out" (as players today call dominating) and show I had major college talent – talent enough as it turned out, to land me in the Brown University Sports Hall of Fame and on the university's 125 Year All-Time Football Team.

The other snub was similar, being undrafted by NFL teams. Rather than discourage me, however, this irritated me and motivated me to make a splash in the CFL – not just to make a team but to show I had NFL talent.

I wasn't happy about playing in a professional league with fewer big-name stars, smaller stadiums, less media coverage and very little American interest overall – something like starring in an off-Broadway play in New York City – so I needed to explode onto the scene and arrive with a bang.

Time would tell if I could pull it off.

CHAPTER TEN:

THE ROAR OF THE CROWD

I could barely hear myself think – or breathe. I was practically hyperventilating.

It was the opening kickoff of the season, commencing our first pre-season game, and everyone in Calgary's McMahon Stadium was standing, stomping and making noise to celebrate the moment.

The decibel levels were rising like thunder as everyone waited for our kicker to charge the ball and kick it deep into enemy territory.

I was on the field in kickoff formation, ready to run through enemy lines, nervous enough to feel like throwing up. It was time to go big or go home.

Finally, our kicker boomed the kick and I was running for my life, laser locked on the return man who caught the ball then dropped it and was trying to grab it as it rolled around near their goal line. While he did that, I blew past one of the opposing blockers assigned to intercept me and continued like a heat-seeking missile toward my target.

The return man now had the ball and was starting up field just as I arrived with a hit that echoed throughout the stadium, like a Cadillac Escalade hitting a Fiat 500 and knocking it sideways and off its wheels. After a half tick of shocked silence, the crowd erupted with a roar as I jumped around celebrating with teammates.

No one could miss me. I was #44, the guy who had just smoked the return man and jump-started the season wearing the number of my earliest childhood hero (Donny Anderson of the Green Bay Packers), a number I had never worn until it was assigned to me in Calgary – a city that now knew my name, thanks to the excited PA announcer.

That crowd watched me make tackles on special teams and on defense all night, including another crowd-pleaser that flipped the opposing punt returner head-over-heels in the air before landing in a big pile of players. The crowd held its breath then roared again and heard my name one more time.

I had arrived with a bang.

THE POWER OF FIRST IMPRESSIONS

After the game I was interviewed on radio, TV and by the newspaper's silver-haired sports reporter. I was also the invited "Player of the Week" at a fan club luncheon with our coaches later that week.

Everyone was eager to learn about the exciting new rookie, where he came from and what he was like. Getting that reaction was both gratifying and fun.

More importantly, the coaches and veteran players looked at me differently after that game. They enjoyed my attitude and energy, and they now respected my ability. I basically made the team right there on the spot, and would soon become their starting middle linebacker, mostly because of that one "splash" performance.

Did I know that at the time? Did I suddenly become overconfident?

Heck no. In fact, the newspaper story that ran the next day featured my answer to the reporter's question about whether I had made the team with my performance.

I told him, "Look, I'm not sure. All I know is that I'll do whatever it takes to make this team. I'll play special teams or play defense or whatever they need. I'll carry water bottles, help the equipment guys or even tape ankles. Whatever it takes!"

He loved my answer, worked it into his headline and treated me like a favorite nephew for as long as I was there.

TAKE IT TO THE BANK

So, what does my Cinderella experience have to do with your impact, success and happiness? Hopefully a lot, even though I wasn't thinking about this topic before we started this chapter. But here we are.

Nobody can make good first impressions all the time, let alone make dramatic show-stopping entrances. Lord knows I've made plenty of bad ones in almost every kind of situation. I'm great at forgetting or mispronouncing names, for instance, or sharing occasionally lame jokes. Not great ways to win friends and influence people!

So, I can't give you a bunch of "First Impression Do's and Don'ts" or even tell you my secrets, even after making another dramatic first game splash the following year after I was traded to Montreal. But more on that later.

I can only *remind you* of what your mother or grandmother probably told you a hundred times since she first combed your hair or tied your ponytail. "You have just one chance to make a first impression!" Right?

Yes, we can all be scared and it's easy to be nervous, but we've got to show the hell up or else we'll be overlooked, ignored and quickly forgotten.

Even if we fail to make a great first impression, we can try again with the second.

We have to stand up straight, fix our gaze on our goal, smile and speak to our potential friend, client, V.I.P. or opportunity and present who the heck we are!

We have to get after it.

You might not hear a roaring crowd, but your spirit will rejoice and your friends and family will say "That's my boy!" or "That's my girl!" I can guarantee you that.

Now let's keep going, because this is getting good, right?

CHAPTER ELEVEN:

A VERY DIFFERENT SPIRIT

Ever seen a bird crash into a window? One minute they're flying along thinking everything looks great then, boom, something invisible stops them cold for a moment before they can recover, flap their wings and fly away.

For me that window was my first pro football camp roommate, Franklin King.

If you saw Franklin, you'd swear he could stop a train cold in its tracks. He stood just about six-feet tall and was built like a refrigerator, like the once famous Chicago Bears star, William "The Refrigerator" Perry.

Like The Fridge, Franklin was a massive defensive nose tackle who had nimble feet and could really move. He also had a big personality.

The day I met Franklin King, I *heard* him before I saw him, as he walked through a lobby full of other players toward our room. He was laughing and joking with everyone as he approached and then discovered me inside.

"Room dog!" he bellowed with a friendly smile as he greeted me, then reached out to shake hands and hug me as teammates do. "My man!"

Franklin was a few years older than me, was already married, had a couple of kids and had spent time playing with another pro team or two. He was there to make the team and feed his family, if he could.

THAT BIG BLACK BOOK

Pre-season days were long and exhausting with early breakfast, followed by meetings, changing into football gear, practice, weights, showers, lunch, a midday break, more meetings, another practice, showers, dinner and sleep.

Waking up was always tough for me, as a notorious night-owl and slow-riser. But I could always count on Franklin to get me going with his singing or inspirational chatter. He was always up early, reading his big black Bible every morning. Same as he did every night before going to bed.

This made Franklin the first person I had ever met, known or witnessed who actually read a Bible outside of a church.

This alone was shocking.

He was also the first person outside of a church building to talk to me about God.

"Yo, room dog," he would say quietly every now and then, usually at night while he was reading and knew I was awake. "You got to know the Lord, man," he would tell me, sometimes in a whisper, choked up or teary-eyed, and always sincerely.

I wasn't offended so much as exposed. Franklin wasn't judging me or even preaching at me. It felt like he could see right through me, ignoring my outward appearance and speaking straight to my soul, and to my true condition.

This made me uncomfortable of course, so I told him I was okay with the Lord (or without him). I didn't dare tell him how I really felt about religion.

WIMPS, WOMEN & POOR PEOPLE

I hated going to church as a kid for several reasons. First and foremost, church services on the West Coast conflicted with the early 10:00 a.m. NFL football games televised from the 1:00 p.m. Eastern time zone.

That was a mortal sin in my book, since video recording or streaming wasn't invented yet. I couldn't tape the games, so they were gone forever.

And if church didn't conflict with football games it still got in the way of surfing with friends on Sunday mornings, when the waves always seemed bigger and better than ever. Glassy with a slight offshore breeze.

Add to those irritations waking up and dressing up to sing hard-to-follow hymns set to outdated organ music, hear boring sermons and suffer through tedious youth classes and you might understand my outlook.

Later when I studied Russian history and learned about communism in college during the Cold War, I read that Karl Marx once called religion "an opiate for the masses." Even though I hated communism I wondered if he was right about that.

I didn't notice much spiritual reality or power in church services or among church people or ministers. It didn't seem very manly, either.

I concluded that religion was a crutch for wimps, women and poor people, and pretty much left it at that.

Now Franklin, as well as several key players on our team, were blowing those thoughts away with a different kind of faith.

They simply had a different spirit – not squeaky-clean or holier-than-thou but pure hearted and powerful. Even sacrificial.

I honestly felt like Franklin King would take a bullet for me. And as much as he wanted and needed to make the team, it felt to me like he would sacrifice his spot for my sake if he needed to.

So, the day I returned to our room and found Franklin cleared out and learned he had been cut from the squad, I felt his loss and his absence deeply. I would miss his bold and uplifting spirit. And I knew his young family would be heartbroken.

Thankfully, Franklin would soon be re-signed and would play again for our team, due to injuries to a few other players. He would get paid to realize his dreams and support his wife and kids. In fact, he would play for several more years.

We would remain supportive teammates, of course, but my roommate time with Franklin, my one and only "room dog," was over. Time would tell what kind of impact he had made on me.

INVASION OF THE BODY SNATCHERS

Later that season an interesting thing happened when one of our practices was cut short to make way for a stadium event scheduled for that evening.

As our team hit the locker room, stadium crews started building a stage on the field and erecting large speakers for some kind of concert.

After showering and getting dressed I went back to the field where a group of our players had pulled chairs out to sit, watch and listen.

As the band warmed up and technicians ran sound checks I watched the crowd arrive and start filling the stadium. But something was different about the people filing inside. They didn't look like concertgoers, or at least they didn't look like rock 'n rollers.

They looked clean-cut and starry-eyed, as if they were being drawn by some invisible force that I could not identify. Like they had a different spirit.

After a minute I turned to the guys and asked, "What the hell is this?"

This got a big laugh out of the group, especially from a couple of older veterans, one of whom replied, "It's the Billy Graham Crusade, dumb ass!"

They all laughed some more as one of the other guys added, "Yeah, you should pull up a chair, brother. See if we can get you saved!"

They laughed some more, and I had to chuckle with them. "Yeah," I said as I turned to leave, "that'll be the day."

CHAPTER TWELVE:

A HONEYMOON SEASON OF STRANGE ENCOUNTERS

I married the cute cheerleader from high school (Suzi is her name) in the church where I was baptized, by the ocean in Palos Verdes Estates, California and we were whisked away from our reception, attended by friends and family from all over the country, in a Rolls-Royce Silver Shadow Sedan borrowed from my rich grandmother (more on her later) and chauffeured by my oldest brother.

The next day we jetted off toward our honeymoon cruise in the Caribbean, followed by a 6-month off-season living by the beach, next to the King Harbor pier in Redondo Beach. All thanks to the football money I had earned and saved and celebrated as a victory won, a risk rewarded, and a dream fulfilled.

That and some generous wedding gifts that certainly didn't hurt.

Suzi worked part-time at a nearby mall to stay busy while I hit the gym or ran sprints every day, studied for my real estate license and worked on writing a screenplay.

Most evenings we would ride, run or roller skate up and down the bike path along the beach, as the sun set over the Pacific.

I didn't know what a "Bullseye Life" was at the time, but that off-season lifestyle sure felt like one.

FUNNY BUSINESS

"Hey John, I'd like to buy you lunch and discuss a business opportunity with you," said George Owens, a friendly, middle-aged and well-connected member of our hometown community. "I want you to meet someone I think you should know – he works in show business and sports and happens to be from Canada – I think you guys might hit it off."

Because of my various interests, this invitation had me hook, line and sinker. So, when the date finally arrived, I was open and eager for opportunity.

Unfortunately, George wanted to present his multi-level marketing (MLM) sales opportunity under the Amway umbrella, a new business model that was growing like wildfire nationwide and earning people some real money at the time.

As an aspiring entrepreneur, I was mildly interested (or at least *politely* interested) in learning more about this unusual business and in supporting George. But I was a little more interested in getting to know George's other lunch guest, Wayne Coombs.

Wayne Coombs was my kind of guy. Jaguar sedan. Expensive suit. Big, friendly and charismatic dude in his early-40s with a client list of famous athletes, authors and celebrities he managed or represented. He also knew CFL football very well as a Toronto native and still played competitive hockey in his spare time.

I didn't believe much in God, but this chance meeting felt like some kind of divine appointment or some kind of special opportunity. So, we exchanged numbers and promised to grab another lunch sometime soon, after our meeting with George ended.

I sensed Wayne might become a key figure in my life the way LA Lakers forward Kermit Washington had become my workout buddy, friend and mentor.

This lunch meeting had spoken to the creative interests I held above and beyond football. Somewhere in my DNA – perhaps from my grandfather John Prassas the commercial real estate developer in Chicago – lurked deep veins of deal-making and business-building instinct. Hence my off-season study for a real estate license and my intense desire to create new business opportunities like the car and boat-detailing business I started with a friend one summer during college.

But just as deep within me were creative passions that had led me to write and submit a book proposal to publishers while in college and currently had me writing a film script with hopes of landing a literary agent – perhaps even someone like Wayne Coombs. After all, he was *in the business!*

PRAYING ON THE PHONE?

My heart was racing with excitement a week later when I arrived to meet Wayne at his office and then go to lunch.

"What a cool cat," I thought to myself as I realized his office was located in the beautiful Malaga Cove Plaza that greets visitors to Palos Verdes Estates who arrive by way of the neighboring Beach Cities. His office was situated upstairs overlooking the Mediterranean plaza's famous Neptune statue and fountain.

This statue of the Greek god of the sea, complete with his mighty trident in hand and surrounded by water-spouting mermaids, was a copy of an ancient bronze statue located in Bologna, Italy that was donated to Palos Verdes in the 1920s by an Italian art dealer who had acquired it from a villa in Venice where it had stood for 100 years.

As a proud Palos Verdes High School graduate and "Sea King," this gave me goosebumps as I hurried into the building and hustled up the stairs to Wayne's office.

Where I had to sit and wait.

Wayne's agency had a small waiting area out front with a receptionist who casually informed me, "You can take a seat, he's just praying on the phone."

A moment later she turned back to me, probably noticing the mystified look on my face. To clarify, she said, "Sometimes he prays with clients or other people in his office but sometimes he just prays on the phone. He's always praying for people."

Just as I considered sprinting out of the building, a door opened, and Wayne stepped into the reception area with arms outstretched and a glowing smile.

"Johnny!" he said, "you ready to eat?!"

I never let anyone but my favorite Great Uncle Nick call me "Johnny," but somehow it felt okay coming from this guy who apparently prayed for people like he was the Pope. So, I gave him thumbs up and we headed out the door.

MOVERS & SHAKERS

As Wayne introduced me to the wonders of calamari at a trendy restaurant in Redondo Beach, he explained that he managed Christian artists and entertainers such as Pat and Debby Boone, Roosevelt Grier, Meadowlark Lemon and a roster of others including the famous automaker John DeLorean and the author Hal Lindsey whose book *Late Great Planet Earth* was selling millions of copies worldwide.

He also spoke matter-of-factly about how God was moving and shaking people everywhere.

One man he knew named John Wimber had gone from being the hell-raising leader of The Righteous Brothers music group to being the laid-back leader of a fast-growing church movement called The Vineyard where they were teaching people to minister to others the way Jesus did and were producing fresh new contemporary worship songs featuring rock music that was starting to sweep the globe.

Another man he knew named Don Tipton had gone from managing the Riviera Country Club in Los Angeles to running freighters loaded with donated medicine, food and other supplies to needy people around the world.

In fact, Don had just told Wayne about a rich Indian shipping magnate who had called him out of the blue to donate a ship to his mercy ministry, saying God woke him up and told him to do it.

The man gave Don Tipton a massive freighter, just like that!

I didn't eat much that day – my jaw was on the floor as I listened in complete shock and awe. I had never heard anyone talk about such amazing things in my life.

After lunch, back at his office, Wayne said he had something for me and then handed me a book. When I looked at the title, I couldn't decide whether to drop it like a scalding hot plate or throw it out the window like some kind of rodent that accidentally fell into my hands. Instead, I just stared at it, paralyzed.

The book was titled *Born Again* by Charles Colson.

Colson had been one of President Nixon's closest White House advisors, hatchet men and Watergate felons who served time in prison before he became a prison reformer and ministry founder, after giving his life to Christ.

"I thought you might be interested," Wayne Coombs said.

"Hell no, I'm not interested!" I screamed silently in my mind as my skin turned hot and probably beet red as I composed myself and said, "Uh, okay, thank you."

Once I noticed Colson was a fellow Brown University graduate, an attorney and a Marine Corp veteran I became mildly interested.

His behind-the-scenes story from inside one of America's great political scandals was right up my alley and seemed weirdly providential. But I wasn't ready to read it.

I had zero interest in religion, so I set it aside as soon as I got home and refused to look at it for a year.

THE GIRL OUT OF NOWHERE

When you live at the beach in Southern California, you're only a couple hours away from the mountains, with peaks like Mt. San Antonio rising up to 10,000-foot elevations. So, when you're looking for adventure or a change of scenery you can make it happen.

One spring day we decided to enjoy some crisp mountain air and hopefully find the perfect make-out spot in the mountains – or at least a nice spot for a picnic – in the Angeles Crest Forest, overlooking LA.

After parking alongside a road in a remote location, miles away from any sign of civilization, we headed up to explore the tall trees, green fields and colorful wildflowers sprawled beneath the cobalt blue sky.

We were like two flower children from the 60s as we walked across a giant field of grass and flowers, totally alone, happy and free to enjoy nature…until a teenage girl appeared out of nowhere up ahead on the barely visible trail we were following and came walking toward us.

As we approached the girl we smiled and said hello as we passed her – with me hoping she wouldn't hang around to cramp our style or spy on us.

She smiled politely and said hello as she passed and continued happily on her way – until she stopped a number of paces later and called back to us.

"Excuse me!" she said, stopping us in our tracks to turn around.

She walked back our way and appeared to be blushing under her freckled nose and cheeks and spoke almost apologetically, yet radiantly at the same time.

"I know this will probably sound strange," she smiled shyly. "But I think God wants you to know that Jesus loves you."

Her words hung in the air for a moment as we absorbed them in shock.

We slowly recovered and thanked her for sharing. Suzi talked with her for a minute while I tried to compose myself, then we continued on our way.

Further up our trail, almost in unison we suddenly looked at each other and laughed out loud, "What the heck was that?!"

I was eager to see what would happen next – preferably on the football field!

CHAPTER THIRTEEN:

HOWEVER FAR YOUR TALENT TAKES YOU

"Why the heck didn't I play today?!" I fumed at our head coach, as I met with him in his office after a pre-season game, during my second season in Calgary.

Never in my life had I stood around in a uniform, watching an entire football game from the sidelines without playing. It was embarrassing and confusing!

"Because we just traded you," he said, happy to offer a somewhat positive answer for me. "Sorry we couldn't play you or tell you with the deal still in the works."

Suddenly everything made sense, but I was still dumbstruck.

"You'll be flying to Montreal tomorrow," he explained, "along with a couple of the other guys."

Everything was changing, thanks to our disappointing season the year before. Our GM had fired our head coach and was now coaching the team himself while trading players and signing free agents. Meanwhile, our former head coach had joined the Montreal staff and was behind the trade for a few of his favorite players, including me.

This trade blindsided me and it would now send us 2,000 miles eastward to Montreal, but that suddenly sparked my competitive spirit and sense of adventure. It also meant another team respected my ability and wanted me in their uniform.

The only problem was that my newlywed bride, Suzi, would have to pack up our newly rented hi-rise apartment overlooking Calgary stadium, load it into a U-Haul trailer and haul it all the way to Montreal – all by herself. Talk about adventure.

FAST-FORWARD

I arrived in Montreal as something of a savior, after giving a spectacular first-impression performance in their final pre-season game just a couple days after I arrived, as they were in dire need of a good middle linebacker they could afford. That's because the team was facing bankruptcy.

Montreal had shocked the sports world a few years earlier by signing top NFL talents like Tom Cousineau, a big-time All-American from Ohio State, as well as LA Rams Super Bowl quarterback Vince Ferragamo and former NFL star receiver Billy "White Shoes" Johnson, the man who pioneered creative touchdown celebrations.

Montreal was attempting to challenge the NFL for top talent, and they still had first round NFL draft picks David Overstreet and Keith Gary on the squad that I joined, but they had failed to convert any of their high-priced talent into winning seasons or increased revenues.

Montreal's Olympic Stadium had looked impressive on TV when it was packed during the 1976 Summer Olympic Games, but it was almost empty for our football games.

Our team went on to lose all but two games in the '82 season, but there were a handful of highlights for me and my wife. One was Brad Blank negotiating a contract extension and signing bonus for me after I threatened to leave because of Quebec's high taxes. Another was having ESPN telecast CFL games in the U.S. when NFL players went on strike that same season. This allowed family and friends to watch my games in the U.S., including two that featured me in post-game interviews after being named Defensive Player of the Game. We also loved the natural beauty, great food and European vibes of Montreal.

The next year in 1983, I missed most of pre-season camp due to tonsillitis and was cut once I returned to action, as the team desperately churned their roster and searched for better players.

Getting sick and then getting cut was discouraging, but I hated losing and playing in front of small home crowds. I also felt like a train-wreck survivor after every game we played on Olympic stadium's infamous Astroturf and rock-hard concrete subfloor.

Thankfully, we heard right away from NFL teams interested in signing me as a free agent, including the Washington Redskins (now Commanders), who had just won the 1983 Super Bowl under head coach Joe Gibbs. Talk about dream destinations.

NEW SEASONS AHEAD

Signing a deal with a Super Bowl winning team loaded with stars like Joe Theismann, Dexter Manley, John Riggins and his celebrated offensive linemen known as "the Hogs," was exciting and uplifting for me, my friends, family and community.

Despite my childhood leg braces, my skinny teenage physique, my Halloween night disaster, my lowly free agent status leaving college and my inglorious release by the CFL's worst team...I was finally reaching the summit, signing a deal and joining the best pro football team in the world.

This felt like a bullseye.

I would now be playing with a team full of Pro Bowlers and world-class athletes, such as their number one draft pick Darrell Green, a collegiate sprint champion and a future Hall of Famer. Green's speed and instincts were obvious from day one, and he would be one of only three new players to make the team's already loaded roster.

In contrast, I didn't make any big hits or "splash" plays. I didn't catch a coach's eye or flash any special talents or potential.

I did okay in drills and scrimmages, but mostly I just struggled with the August heat and humidity – and suffered every day from sleep deprivation, thanks to a crappy old AC unit that barely worked in my dorm room. This wore me down like the massive offensive linemen I faced every day in practice, as I tossed and turned every night.

In that place and time, I just didn't shine or stand out.

So, when they knocked on my door, told me I was cut and sent me home, I wasn't surprised or heartbroken. I was simply exhausted.

The lessons I learned were simple. The higher the level of excellence, the shorter your window of opportunity. The more talented (or well-established) your competition, the more dynamic you need to be. And as usual, the better your first impression, the better your chances of opening doors.

I had pushed my physical talent as far as it could take me.

Now, as I made the long flight home, I was disappointed yet proud of my journey. I was proud of where I had come from and how far I had come.

Instead of tears, however, I had a new gleam in my eye.

Key elements of my history, dreams and DNA were colliding and converging as I looked out the window toward a new and different kind of season ahead.

My eye was on a billion-dollar idea.

CHAPTER FOURTEEN:

RE-SETTING YOUR SIGHTS

"**V**CR sales have doubled again and there's no end in sight," I told the prospective investors, as I walked them through my business plan in 1984. "Everyone is renting videos, but no one wants to stand in line at crowded video stores," I assured them.

When my football life ended my entrepreneurial life began. It was in my family history, dreams and DNA. Or so I thought, anyway.

I had run a business back in high school (the Key Club Christmas tree lot) and created one during college (a car and boat detailing service), but now I was presenting a serious business plan to serious investors to raise serious money for a business with billion-dollar potential. A friend of mine had helped me develop the plan as part of his MBA program at USC, so it was no joke.

My idea was to launch a video delivery service called *VIP Video Express* to busy professionals working in the high-rise office towers of downtown Los Angeles, knowing they could order quickly by phone and pay just a couple extra bucks for the convenience of taking videos straight home and back to their office, without having to stop at retail stores. And if it worked in one big city it could work in others, so we might need to expand quickly.

We had researched the video rental market, collected wholesale pricing and contacts, prepared reasonable P&L projections and marketing plans, and even found inexpensive office space downtown. Demand was a given. Delivery logistics were budgeted. I had a small but talented staff, led by a friend who was ready to go. It was a compelling pitch.

DECISIONS, DECISIONS

What followed were a series of bad decisions that could have been avoided by reviewing the plan through the lens of personal convergence.

The first bad decision was mine.

I had fallen in love with my trend-savvy concept and its massive market potential without recognizing how long it might take to get the new business model off the ground or how heavy the management demands might be; of actively operating the day-to-day operations to prove the concept, of buying and selling inventory, handling deliveries, managing customer service and marketing all at once. I didn't have that experience or the right (administrative) DNA to tackle it – even with the investor's support and partial involvement.

The second bad decision was made by the investors.

They should have recognized that my impressive business plan, presentation skills, market acumen and research could not compensate for my total lack of experience in a high-volume, low-margin delivery business or in video retailing.

As it turned out, our market launch was successful in that people loved the service. Unfortunately, they all wanted the same new movies on the same weekends, when peak demand came and went quickly (before covering the cost of those hot titles) and very few customers wanted to rent the library titles we bought to complement the new releases and add income.

We couldn't feed the beast or scale it up without burning an indefinite about of money, so our investor pulled the plug after six months and I couldn't blame him.

My epic business venture was an epic fail.

A few years later, another video delivery service offered DVDs sent to your home mailbox and figured out how to fund and scale it. Their name was Netflix, and they have obviously come a long way from shipping DVDs in the mail. Today they're valued at $214 billion.

PASSIONS & DISTRACTIONS

It's hard to aim at multiple targets at the same time. In fact, it's impossible.

Sure, you can have secondary interests, but keeping your goals and commitments primary is essential but often difficult.

To give a big YES commitment to one thing, you have to say NO to many other things to be successful.

During this "post-football" period of my life, I had to learn this the hard way.

As a pro athlete, other interests were obviously secondary to playing or training for my sport. This meant screenwriting, real estate or other creative or entrepreneurial interests knew their place and time – on the side, during the off-season or in the future. But without that supreme focal point, I was now vulnerable to distraction.

While formulating and operating the video delivery business, for instance, I had to sort through multiple opportunities, commitments, and distractions.

1. My Hollywood literary agent was pitching my first script around town and was asking if I had another one. So, I was writing in my spare time.

2. A rock 'n roll band called me out of the blue and asked if I could produce an MTV music video for them. After confirming their budget and the willingness of two film industry friends to help me, I said yes. This led to scouting and negotiating locations, scriptwriting, equipment rentals, rehearsals, casting, location shoots and editing – all in my spare time.

3. Legendary acting coach Vince Chase, who I met casually through a friend taking his classes, invited me to join his evening workshops on Sunset Blvd. He even offered to waive my tuition when I told him I couldn't swing it. At his insistence, I agreed to try but had to quit after a few weeks. He was eager to launch my acting career, but I was committed to launching a business. I couldn't do both.

4. And finally, there was my wife, Suzi, who deserved my *prime time,* rather than my spare time – both of which were in short supply.

These competing interests didn't cause the video business to fail, but they certainly didn't help.

A TIME TO RECOVER

How do you deal with a loss, failure, or disappointment when you thought you were on the verge of something great, like a billion-dollar concept that goes down in flames?

Hopefully, you can find a safe place to recover, re-focus and simplify your life. You can also try to pay closer attention to the signs and signals of convergence.

For me this meant taking a corporate job at a Fortune 500 company just down the road near LAX, at The Garrett Corporation.

My job was to assist the head of corporate communications, which involved advertising, PR, trade shows and more, frequently working with top executives, important vendors and traveling to air shows or industry events as part of a small "swat team" group of specialists.

These specialists were fun guys and talented professionals who managed to stay under the radar, get their work done and play lots of golf on company time. They often socialized (and enjoyed free meals and drinks) with thankful vendors who they hired to build expensive booths and displays for the company or to ship precious cargo like jet engine cut-aways, turbo displays or double-decker booth materials to and from events.

This was a fun and easy dream job! If you were wired for it.

But before we address my particular "wiring," let me applaud the value of a stable and respectable job with benefits. It can be a glorious thing!

In this case, my job was bullet-proof and nicely aligned with my interests in advertising, PR and communications. I was working in a long-established and well diversified company serving the aerospace and automotive industries, just 25 minutes from home. I had job security, a healthy income and solid health benefits. It was a perfect place to recover.

This stable period allowed me and my wife to buy a cute little mid-century "fixer" home in a great neighborhood and to have a baby without financial or emotional stress. It was a good solid place to work hard, learn about business, experience corporate culture and focus on my family and our home life.

There was a downside, however, and I just referred to it as corporate culture. For me and my temperament, that culture would become toxic.

The corporate culture felt too tightly regulated, too limited, too confined to your level or specific task. It seemed closed-minded, repetitive, too comfortable and too 9-to-5. Plus, I didn't play golf or drink more than an occasional beer. So the perks of my position were not attractive to me.

One time, when I reviewed the company's promotional giveaway (swag) budgets and reported that we could save thousands by diversifying our sources, I was told not to worry about it, out of loyalty to our existing vendor.

When I watched fellow employees leave early, avoid work or take advantage of company expense accounts, it made me uncomfortable – not as some kind of whistle-blower, but as someone who expects more hustle and commitment from people toward their job and organization. I didn't want to be (or feel like) a slacker.

With all that said, one thing was for sure. I wasn't going to leave that job and jeopardize that stability for any "hot concept" or half-baked scheme, situation or opportunity, just to escape the 9-to-5 or to regain my sense of adventure.

WHEN CONVERGENCE CALLS

That's when my hometown buddy Andy Bark called.

Andy was a fellow Palos Verdes Sea King just a couple years behind me in school who had played wide receiver at the Air

Force Academy and then at Cal, after concussions he suffered while playing voided his ability to fly jets and allowed him to transfer. After excelling at Cal, he played briefly in the USFL and with the San Diego Chargers.

Now Andy lived in a small apartment on the beach, where he delivered daily surf reports to LA radio stations, played lots of beach volleyball and networked with *everyone*, as one of the most likeable and well-connected people on earth.

Since he had recently starred in the music video I produced (while also helping to cast and organize the project), and had seen my business plan and related efforts for the video business, he wanted to bounce a business idea off of me.

"I want to publish something like *Texas Football Magazine*," he said, "but for California." He let the idea sink in, then said, "I think we can make it bigger and better."

He had been inspired by the Texas magazine's rabid following by Texas athletes he had played with and by a conversation he had had with Rupert Murdoch, the global publishing tycoon he had met through his actor friend Christopher Atkins, while filming *The Blue Lagoon* in Australia. That's when Murdoch had recommended publications to Andy as one of the world's greatest businesses to own and operate.

Andy told me he had an investor interested but he needed a business plan and some additional talent, passion and experience to win the investor's support and to create such a publication.

Would I be interested in partnering?

Thus began our brainstorming and business development plans for *California Football Magazine,* and all that it might become.

My only demand, other than a fair ownership split, was a salary that matched my corporate position at Garrett. I couldn't afford to be a starving entrepreneur with a wife, new baby, and a mortgage to pay at home.

Meanwhile, my one concern was whether the investor would give us enough time to build the business while incurring losses during the startup and growth phases.

And so, we got started working on a business plan and proposal and presented it like pros. After we won the investor's commitment, I left Garrett and we hit the ground running.

Was I crazy to jump back into the entrepreneurial fire, or was I watching personal convergence unfold again?

It certainly felt like a bullseye to me, with its amazing mix of creativity, teamwork, leadership, sales, marketing, design and nonstop communications work – all in the sports field of my greatest dreams and achievements.

And there was even more.

I was even more impressed by the convergence I saw happening in Andy Bark's life. And this is one of the most important keys I like to share and emphasize.

If you're going to work with someone or for someone (whether an individual or an organization), you need to study and assess their history, dreams and DNA. Is there harmony, alignment and power visible, if not on full display with them? Is there something special or dynamic at work, generating heat and momentum in and around them?

I saw those dynamics at work in Andy's life.

So, when Nike founder Phil Knight became one of our first subscribers and struck up a friendly relationship with Andy, I was not surprised.

I was pretty sure we were on a speeding rocket ship. We would have to see where it would take us.

CHAPTER FIFTEEN:

HISTORY'S BIGGEST BULLSEYE

When Troy Aikman walked into the room, I thought to myself, *Dang, this kid looks like a linebacker not a quarterback.*

He stood about 6'3" and 225 pounds and immediately conveyed a no-nonsense vibe suggesting he was more of a ranch hand or oil worker from Henryetta, Oklahoma than a handsome QB born and raised in Orange County, California. But he was both.

You didn't know that Troy would soon become the NFL's #1 draft pick, a three-time Super Bowl champion and Hall of Famer for the Dallas Cowboys – or a Fox Sports TV commentator and the eventual face of ESPN's *Monday Night Football*. But you could tell there was something special about him.

Troy was probably more apprehensive that day than usual, after driving across town from UCLA to USC's Heritage Hall – straight into the heart of his crosstown rival's territory – to join us for our second annual *California Football Magazine* Kick-Off edition cover shoot.

This was where he would have to pose with USC quarterback Rodney Peete and Los Angeles Mayor Tom Bradley. Thankfully,

UCLA's Sports Information Director knew it would be good press, so he promised that Troy would be there.

Troy and Rodney would face each other and grip hands like arm-wrestlers, wearing their Cardinal Red and Powder Blue home jerseys, with Mayor Bradley standing behind them like a referee. They would grin for the camera, producing a classic shot and another promotional "win" for our publication, complete with interviews and stories about both players.

The year before our cover had introduced a high school linebacker named Junior Seau, a freakish athlete who wowed us with his positive energy that lit up the room. Meanwhile, I was working to arrange a photo shoot with the national record-breaking high school quarterback, Todd Marinovich, to have him pose with an F-15 fighter jet, courtesy of the good people at El Toro Air Force Base, near his home.

We were working hard, being creative and making waves.

BUSINESS MODEL BATTLES

After careful study we decided to launch a different kind of magazine. It would be larger than normal – tabloid size – with color covers for visual impact and mostly black and white photos and copy on newsprint paper inside, to limit print costs.

To maximize readership interest, we would cover all 1,200-plus high schools, 70-plus junior colleges, 30-plus colleges/universities and all four pro teams in the state, in one way, shape or form, through team and league summaries, stats, interviews and stories, with as many player and coach names mentioned as possible.

We would write certain features ourselves (like Peete and Aikman) with most other content submitted or collected by field editors or contributors throughout the state, led by

California state sports "gurus" and team members, Mark and Nelson Tennis.

To maximize our circulation and reach our target demographic (kids, coaches and their families) and to give sufficient appeal to potential advertisers, we chose to distribute 100,000 copies directly to teams at strategic times of the year, for FREE. This is commonly known as controlled circulation, with paid subscriptions offered but not relied upon for calculating ad rates.

If you think this sounds like a lot of work, you're right. If you think this sounds expensive, you are also correct!

Selling ads and sponsorships would quickly become our greatest pressure point. And *successfully* selling ads would be a non-stop battle. So we were hitting the phones every day and flying all over the country to meet and present to potential clients.

While most advertisers loved our publications (which soon included *California Basketball Magazine)*, with our huge California state market and desirable demographics, some wanted to "wait and see" if we survived long enough to earn their trust or they needed to wait for their next budget cycle to consider it. And still others thought we were too small or too infrequently published (or both) to even mess around with us.

Thankfully there were plenty of large advertisers and sponsors (or their ad agencies) who wanted to participate, but they often had only national budgets or local budgets to work with – not regional or statewide budgets that fit our opportunity.

This applied to numerous "no-brainer" companies that sold soft drinks, sports drinks, fast food, sports apparel, candy, gaming and shoes, to name just a few.

This reality put us in a bind and forced us to work even harder and more creatively to win the occasional movie release, armed forces recruitment ad or athletic shoe contract.

After three years of hitting these same walls, I was finally determined to present an expansion plan for us to raise more capital from the agents, pro athletes and other investors we knew were already interested in our company, to roll our business into other parts of the country and to form a *national brand.*

This would grow our company, relieve our financial pressure, meet the requirements of our national advertisers and keep us ahead of new competitors entering the market, all in one fell swoop.

So at our next meeting with our investor, I presented the plan, confident it was a super smart move – if not genius.

What I didn't appreciate was how our investor might feel about diluting his majority ownership share (and losing his total control) of the company to make room for other investors, after he had invested so much in the company.

But I can tell you now that he *hated* it!

He lost his temper, called me a quitter and demanded that I leave the company.

MY ROCK 'N ROLL SAVIOR

I decided to wipe the proverbial "dust off my feet" and walk away rather than fight, sue or squabble. At this point I was tired of hitting the same wall and thinking small, and I didn't want to hurt my partner, Andy, by messing things up any further.

If we couldn't (or wouldn't) take our concept nationwide and fulfill its potential, I was no longer interested. Another friend wanted me to help him launch a national publication for marketing commercial real estate, so I would do that instead.

Meanwhile, I had become a lot more interested in hanging out with Jesus.

I had read *Born Again*, the book Wayne Coombs had given me a few years earlier, along with a classic called *More Than a Carpenter* and even the book by Wayne's client and friend Hal Lindsey, *The Late Great Planet Earth*, back when I was still playing football.

Meanwhile, Suzi and I had continued to encounter seemingly supernatural people and situations, including a rock 'n roll Easter service organized by Wayne Coombs at the high school gym on top of the hill in Palos Verdes, a quarter mile away from where I was brought home from the hospital, as a baby.

Hal Lindsey was the speaker that day, but rather than talk about ancient prophecies relating to current events around the world (per his bestselling book), he gave a detailed historical account of Jesus' triumphal entry, trial, execution and resurrection. It blew my mind and overwhelmed my spirit. When he asked if anyone wanted to receive Jesus by faith, Suzi and I went forward in tears.

What finally won me over to Christ wasn't hellfire and brimstone, religious guilt or my need for a crutch.

I simply saw Jesus for who he is – not some religious figure with weird hats and robes or rules and regs, but a totally cool, down to earth and very real man, yet totally divine and supernatural at the same time. I sensed his love and forgiveness for every wrong thing I'd ever done wrong, felt his renewing spirit and heard his invitation to join him on an adventure greater than anything I could muster on my own.

So, I bowed my heart, said okay, and cried my eyes out for twenty minutes.

It felt like spiritual convergence.

THE STUBBORN KID WITH THE SLING

A handful of years later I was the 33-year-old pastor of a church that met in a rock 'n roll nightclub facility on Pacific Coast Highway, just a few blocks from the beach.

I had earned a master's degree at Fuller Theological Seminary in Pasadena, CA after leaving the business world for what I called a "season of study." But I was a lot more interested in seeing our church members bring food, music and fellowship to the homeless and destitute people on Skid Row in San Pedro or provide hands-on help to drug babies needing foster care or to touch and pray for regular folks needing miracles, than talking about theology. So that's what we were doing.

Our Sunday meetings at the popular bar and concert venue were intended to open doors to "sinners and outcasts" who might want to hear contemporary worship music and experience the love of Jesus without walking into a traditional church.

One day I was studying at our nearby office preparing my Sunday message, studying the story of David and Goliath, when I noticed something so clear and obvious it practically slapped me in the face.

Holy moly, I thought to myself. *There it is!*

I couldn't help but notice that David's personal history, dreams and DNA converged on the day he stubbornly refused to go home or back down from the giant Philistine warrior, Goliath, in the famous story most people have heard a thousand times.

I was utterly amazed as I looked through the lens of personal convergence.

I instantly recognized David was the "poster child for personal convergence," as the best-known person in history to demonstrate its power. I then considered the stone he sent whistling into Goliath's forehead as history's biggest bullseye.

As I looked closer at David's story, I noticed seven key background areas that stood out as important markers, helping us to see how convergence combines and incorporates critical elements from every part of our lives – whether we are Bible heroes, hi-tech billionaires or anything in between.

So, let's look at those key elements and see how they apply to us and where they might take you and me.

CHAPTER SIXTEEN:

YOUR CONVERGENCE QUIZ

As we move forward to explore David's 7 Keys let's quickly tackle another quiz to test your comprehension and to encourage your application of the recent chapters.

Here again you have multiple-choice questions, plus a simple essay question. You know the drill so here you go:

1. Chasing your dream can be:

    A. Exhilarating to pursue and achieve

    B. Lonely and a bit scary

    C. The ultimate test of your faith and commitment

    D. Painful if you fail or fall short

    E. All the above

2. Making a "splash" or good first impression is:

    A. Too risky to attempt

    B. Almost a "must" for achieving certain goals

    C. What your mother told you to do

    D. Both B and C

3. Spiritual matters should be:

A. Ignored or rejected

B. Kept private and never shared

C. Considered a supernatural part of life

D. Freely shared with others you care about

E. Part of seeking your ultimate destiny

4. The lesson learned here about talent is:

A. It plays a major role in how far or high you go

B. Talent doesn't matter, it's all about your effort

C. It takes hard work and commitment to maximize it

D. Both A and C

5. When you fulfill your dream (or let it go) you should:

A. Celebrate in the U.S. Virgin Islands

B. Post your most hilarious happy dance on TikTok

C. Re-set your sights on a new dream, goal or vision

D. Quit, "fold your tent," and call it a day

6. Personal convergence is:

A. A concept discovered on Mars

B. Similar to nuclear fusion

C. When multiple aspects of your life powerfully merge

D. Both B and C

7. When it comes to distractions or conflicting interests:

   A. You don't worry if you're super talented

   B. You write them down, then burn the paper

   C. You know they can exhaust and defeat you

   D. You know a big YES commitment requires other NO's

   E. Both C and D

8. Before you work for or with others or launch your own thing:

   A. You should eat a nutritious breakfast

   B. You should run a credit check and meet with the FBI

   C. You should confirm positive signs of convergence

9. Essay Question: Which of the last group of stories can you relate with the most, and why? Anything else catch your attention or speak to your situation? Take a moment to write down your answer, jot down notes or just reflect in your own mind. And feel free to share your thoughts with me at essays@HitYourBullseye.com.

ANSWER KEY

   1. E – Yup, chasing dreams is not for the faint of heart.

   2. D – Yes, you've got to go for it!

   3. X – The correct answer is in the eye of the beholder on this one, but I recommend C, D & E.

   4. D – Yes, talent matters. We'll be looking at gifts, talents and skills ahead.

5. C – The other choices might work, but a re-set is usually required.

6. D – This is a repeat question to make sure you got it.

7. E – Yes, we need to focus on the main thing.

8. C – Yes, you want to harness the power!

9. Go to essays@hityourbullseye.com if you'd like to share.

Now let's turn the page and check out those keys…

PART II:

THE 7 KEYS

CHAPTER SEVENTEEN:

KEY #1: YOUR FAMILY HISTORY

You can read the full story of David and Goliath in the Bible's book of I Samuel, but David's story – like ours – began with his family, and it unfolded this way.

David was the youngest of eight brothers and was just a teenager when his father sent him to deliver food from their farm to his older brothers on the front lines of a battlefield where the army of Israel was facing an army of Philistines, with a valley stretched between them, roughly 3,000 years ago.

The armies had held their positions in a stalemate for some time, with only the Philistine's giant-sized champion Goliath stepping forward each day to taunt the Israelites and challenge them to present a warrior for a one-on-one winner-take-all battle between him and whoever they dared send to face him.

When David arrived, he was greatly troubled to learn that no Israelite would fight the giant, especially after hearing that a great reward (marriage to the king's daughter and the wealth that came with it) had been offered by Israel's King Saul to anyone who would fight and defeat the Philistine.

Goliath's massive body, huge weapons, heavy armor and trash-talking arrogance had paralyzed the entire Israelite army with fear.

David was also offended by Goliath's taunts and blasphemy hurled at the soldiers and God of Israel, each day. He was fighting mad about the whole situation and was also intrigued by the king's reward. So, he kept asking around the ranks of soldiers, trying to confirm that the reward was real.

David's actions upset his oldest brother, Eliab, who accused him of shirking his duties at home just to hang around and watch the battle. Eliab's anger was no doubt fueled by his jealousy toward David, something we will discuss a little later.

Like so many younger siblings, David ignored his older brother and kept asking about the king's reward until he was brought to stand before King Saul, where he offered to fight the giant.

Saul admired the lad's willingness to fight but dismissed his chances due to his youth, size, and inexperience. But David assured the king that he had killed both a lion and a bear while shepherding his family's sheep and he assured Saul he could do the same with Goliath.

King Saul was impressed by David's confidence. He offered David his own personal armor, bronze helmet and other weaponry to use in battle, but David declined, knowing they didn't fit his body or his tactics. Instead, David chose five stones out of a creek, grabbed his sling and headed out to meet Goliath.

When the giant laid eyes on David he scoffed, taunted, and cursed the young man, promising to feed his dead flesh to the birds of the air and beasts of the field.

David countered with words that have stirred the hearts of believers for centuries, saying, "You come to me with sword, spear and javelin but I come to you in the name of the Lord, the God of Israel whom you have defiled." Then, with righteous anger and adrenaline coursing through his veins, David delivered a bold promise.

"Today the Lord will deliver you into my hands and I will smite you and cut off your head," he declared. "Then I will give the corpses of your Philistine army to the birds and beasts so that all the earth should know that there is a God in Israel – and everyone will know that the Lord saves not with sword and spear, for the battle is the Lord's and He will give you into our hands."

Furious, Goliath moved to engage David who loaded his sling, ran forward and launched his stone toward the giant, hitting him smack in the forehead, dropping him face down in the dust. David quickly moved to Goliath's fallen body, grabbed the giant's sword and did what he had promised to do – causing the Philistine army to flee in fear, chased by the Israelites until their victory was complete.

And so, the story of David and Goliath goes, complete with family drama, trash talk, a clutch performance and even some blood and guts.

TIME & PLACE

In the context of personal convergence, there are numerous elements related to your family history, starting with where you came from and when you arrived.

David was born near Bethlehem in Judah, Israel, circa 1000 BC, in a time and place of ongoing warfare over control of the Promised Land. His family farmed and bred sheep and they were proud and prominent members of the tribe of Judah.

To create his hallmark moment in history, David had to be born and raised in the appropriate time and place, and live among people who diligently recorded their history.

Another Bible hero, the beautiful queen Esther, who saved her people from genocide 700 years later, was said to be "born for a time such as this," reinforcing the convergent qualities of time, place and destiny.

In more recent history, Henry Ford was born and raised within reach of Detroit Michigan during the Industrial Revolution, where he could work at Emerson Electric and rub shoulders with top engineers, before starting the Ford Motor Company and building cars that changed the world.

Today's General Motors CEO Mary Barra was also born and raised in Michigan, where her father worked at a GM (Pontiac) factory, which positioned her for a job inspecting hoods and fenders at 18 and for earning her engineering degree through the General Motors Institute. That accomplishment, in turn, positioned her for graduate study at Stanford University and for the series of GM management and executive positions that followed.

Steve Jobs grew up during the digital revolution and lived near today's Silicon Valley in the Bay Area of California, where he was able to call local resident Tom Hewlett, the CEO and founder of Hewlett Packard, to request a computer part and land a part-time job at the age of 13, then later started Apple Computer in his family's garage.

In contrast to these "homegrown" examples and to illustrate what many immigrants and dream-seekers have known for years about *changing* your time and place, we can look at Tesla CEO and Space-X founder Elon Musk, today's richest man in the world.

Though he was born and raised in South Africa, Musk was determined to make his way to North America, first to Canada through his family ties, then on to the University of Pennsylvania to study physics and economics and finally on to Standford University for graduate study, which he dropped almost immediately to join the digital boom centered in the San Francisco Bay Area, where he started his first tech company.

Time and place were clearly important to me, as well. My upbringing in Southern California positioned me to play high school football in a highly competitive and talent-rich area where I could easily be discovered and recruited by colleges. It was also a natural place to meet or know entertainment professionals, which eventually enabled me to produce music videos and TV commercials, write for Disney and co-found an Emmy Award-winning sports media company.

Was I a product of my environment or just fortunate to seize local opportunities aligned with my interests? Either way I was clearly affected by my time and place.

How about you? Where are you from? And how did your time and place of origin shape, prepare or position you? Did you embrace the unique qualities or opportunities of your hometown or your family's roots? Or did you seek to branch out from them, or even escape them altogether? Connect the dots where you can.

FAMILY TRAITS & TRADITIONS

When we go to the doctor, we're normally asked about our family history. This can be a sobering reminder of just how connected we are to our families, and how those connections can be literal "life and death" background factors.

In most families there are strong "genetic codes" at work, as well as physical, social and spiritual traits, ties, proclivities and value systems, with unique family tales of success, failure, heartbreak, pride and more.

David's family history and values went back to Moses and beyond, all the way to Abraham, the Father of the Hebrew nation. This gave David a strong sense of identity, purpose and pride. He knew who he was and 'where he came from.'

He was also the great grandson of Bible heroes Ruth and Boaz who became famous for their loyalty, sacrifice and kindness by going above and beyond their call of duty to help others in need. Ruth and Boaz's acts ultimately brought them together in marriage and gave David and his family a pair of noble history-making heroes to follow.

As noted in this book's Introduction, my Greek immigrant grandfather advanced from selling fruit baskets and flowers on busy street corners in Chicago to building shopping centers and living in a mansion overlooking Lake Michigan. And though I didn't get to see him very often due to distance and strained relationships, his example (or genetic traits) somehow influenced me and my brothers to pursue significant real estate development projects and/or real estate brokerage activities over the years, even while working in other professions.

My other grandfather traveled the world as a merchant seaman, which could explain my love of travel and my zest for adventure.

My grandmothers presented very different stories and traits. One was a deeply religious woman who raised my mother and her siblings alone while her husband sailed the seven seas. The other one lived like a movie star after divorcing my Greek grandfather in Chicago and moving to Los Angeles, where she married a rich industrialist who died and left her a fortune.

This grandmother drove a Rolls Royce, rocked massive diamonds, raced thoroughbreds, lived two doors up from the *Beverly Hillbillies* mansion (in the hills of Bel-Air) and traveled the world – in route to burning through her millions.

Beyond this eccentric mixture of family traits and history, my immediate family was built, above all other things, on a high regard for education. My father attended his dream college of Northwestern on the GI Bill after serving in World War II (and later earned a master's degree in aerospace engineering at USC), while my mother put herself through college in just three years at Cal-Berkeley.

These family values have now become a family legacy as multiple generations of our family have studied at Ivy League and/or other top-ranked universities.

My regard for higher education comes with one very important caveat, however.

I have always respected "street smarts" as much as "book smarts," and have enjoyed working with talented and hard-working contractors, mechanics, artists and craftspeople no matter what their "formal" education might be.

This respect was greatly reinforced by my wife's parents who built a steel forging empire without any college diplomas or advanced degrees. Her father was a high-school drop-out, in fact, who joined the Merchant Marines at 16 (lying about his age to get in), to serve his country and to escape his painful family background.

Fortunately, my father-in-law possessed a genius for working with steel and later built record-breaking race cars as a side hobby. My mother-in-law was also smart, great with numbers and tough enough to sell steel and run the company long before women had ascended to such leadership positions – especially in such blue-collar industries.

They both possessed a "fire in their belly" to succeed and they credited that as their ultimate X-factor for success.

These are a few of my family traits and traditions. There are other less positive traits and dynamics present in most families, as well, based on tragic losses, mistakes, fears, painful experiences and more.

My parents greatly preferred "security" over risk, for instance, due to their painful experiences growing up in the Great Depression (and watching their own parents cope) and they tended to "play it safe," as a result. My brothers and I had to challenge those traits to pursue our more entrepreneurial dreams.

What are your family traits and traditions?

What values, themes or expectations prevailed in your family? Which achievements were most highly valued? What pursuits were seen as most important and expected? Was it education, business, hard work, recreation, adventure, religion, sports or something else?

Does your family have a proud history of military service, medicine, law enforcement, teaching or something else that has shaped, attracted or fueled you? Or is there some negative history you must overcome to reach your goals and re-direct your family's social, spiritual or financial trajectory?

BIRTH ORDER

David's birth order as the youngest of eight sons was certainly significant, given the privilege and abuse that so often accompanies that position. With seven older brothers (and two sisters), David may have felt special as the "baby of the family," but he probably developed a mind of his own and a chip on his shoulder to prove himself, as well; critical factors that were on display when he stepped forward to fight Goliath.

How different would his response to Goliath have been if he was a practical, "bossy" or brilliant firstborn child? Or how about a mellow, peacemaking or "frustrated" middle child? Birth-order traits don't always hold true to form but they can influence our life's trajectory and help determine our most comfortable roles in groups, organizations and relationships.

As the youngest child in my family, I can certainly appreciate David's stubborn streak, feisty attitude and almost compulsive drive to prove himself and take action – even when it looks dangerous or crazy!

Kylie Jenner's birth order position in the world-famous Kardashian family provides yet another interesting insight into birth-order traits, challenges and opportunities.

In her case, like most younger siblings, Kylie could watch and learn from her older siblings' glaring setbacks and mistakes while also working to leverage and build upon their successes, all while bringing her own unique history, dreams and DNA to the party. This is now manifested through Kylie's billion-dollar cosmetics and lifestyle company and her global online following. None of it was possible without her extraordinary family background, yet it's all uniquely created by her.

As you consider your birth order, can you see how it affects your social outlook, challenges and opportunities? And your personal "comfort zone?"

Lots of firstborn children naturally lead and manage others because it often comes with their childhood "job description" of herding their siblings. This is one reason roughly 50% of corporate CEOs are firstborn children.

For similarly obvious reasons, middle children are often more easy-going and agreeable peacemakers, diplomats and therapists – or tortured souls who feel boxed in or overlooked by those around them, sometimes leading to deeper reflection, rebellion and/or artistry and self-expression.

Youngest children, like David, can be scene-stealing risk-takers and are often outgoing and fun-loving, according to birth-order experts – and even casual observers.

Where did you fit into your family dynamic? And how do you now fit most impactfully, successfully and happily in whatever setting you find yourself or *seek* to find yourself? These are questions to keep in mind, and dynamics to harness if you can.

THE NAME GAME

David's name means "beloved" in Hebrew, and it resonates with the Bible's reference to him as "a man after God's own heart." His name expressed his parent's heart for him at birth, perhaps sensing his special calling or favor to come.

Queen Esther's name, meanwhile, was based on the Babylonian goddess Ishtar which translated roughly to "star." Her starring role in a historic life or death drama affecting her captive nation was certainly fitting.

Names can reflect family history, aspirations or creativity and they can prove to be prophetic, pointing us toward our ultimate destiny, or influencing our sense of identity or purpose in some way.

Martin Luther King Jr., for instance, was originally named *Michael* King Jr., but was re-named by his father at the age of five, when his father changed his own name as well. His father, a notable church leader in Atlanta, GA, visited Germany in 1934 where he was so disturbed by the rise of Adolph Hitler and Naziism and so inspired by the story of Martin Luther, the humble monk who sought to reform the corrupt and legalistic church in medieval Europe, that he changed their names to Martin Luther. He hoped that he and his son would somehow make an impact similar to their namesake.

I was named after my grandfather, the Chicago developer, and my name John means "God has been graceful," to which I must say "Amen." Without a double dose of grace, my life story would be very different – and much more difficult.

My middle name Nicholas, meanwhile, honors my favorite great uncle Nick, a charismatic and sports-minded man who inspired me. I admired his sense of style, his upbeat attitude and his beautiful beachfront condo in Fort Lauderdale, Florida! As a result, I often use my middle name when I write or do business, knowing it means both "overcomer" and "victory for the people" in the ancient Greek.

These ancient translations inspire me and resonate with my core values and experiences. They also prompt me to share their meanings with others with the same name, often inspiring them in the process.

So, how about you? Were you named after someone in your family or to honor someone, something or someplace special or famous? Does your name mean something meaningful in its root language? Your name obviously shapes your identity and can be a factor in your life experience and sense of destiny – even if you have to change it, as so many leaders, artists and others have over the years, to become the person you are destined to be.

YOUR FAMILY HISTORY & TRAJECTORY

Your family's history has shaped, directed and influenced you. It may have even positioned and launched you in a certain trajectory, for good or bad, happy or sad. But the rest is up to you.

David harnessed the power of his family history in a unique and personal way that represented his background yet introduced a new and different trajectory based on his unique destiny.

This is your opportunity and your challenge, as well.

Your task is to ponder, pray, review and reflect on these family matters, and on whatever thoughts, memories or insights come with them. Connect your dots, recognize patterns and keep them in mind as we look toward your ultimate trajectory.

Thankfully, there's a lot more to David's epic bullseye experience, and more to yours as well. So, let's get into more of it!

CHAPTER EIGHTEEN:

KEY #2: YOUR PERSONALITY TRAITS

Everyone is hard-wired with various personality traits; you, me and David, too.

So, it pays to understand these traits as much as we can, for our own sake and for the sake of others around us (I'll share why in a minute). But good luck trying to sort them all out or nail them all down because personality traits are still a bit of a mystery.

Parents have marveled over the years, in fact, at how different their children's personalities can be despite sharing the very same gene pool and upbringing, and how Matthew or Madison were simply "born happy" or stubborn or outgoing or independent or whatever traits describe them.

These traits often blur with the birth-order characteristics we discussed last chapter, but they almost always define us throughout our lives and determine much about our life direction, "best fit" and ultimate happiness.

So, they do warrant our attention, and they do stand out in our case study.

When David arrived on his historic "bullseye" battlefield scene, he showcased a number of obvious traits we can identify and learn from.

Just consider a few questions. Did David exhibit a forceful reaction to the Goliath situation or a contemplative one? Did he look to others for emotional support or was he self-confident and independent? Was he more of a "good soldier" or a "take charge" type of teenager? Was he submissive and compliant to the rules and restrictions around him or defiant and innovative – or even a little of both?

You get the idea.

Clearly, David showed himself to be assertive or "dominant," which are typical traits of leadership. He was influential enough to persuade King Saul, non-compliant enough to ignore his brother and reject traditional weapons, and yet submissive enough to seek "official approval" rather than just run out to battle Goliath on his own.

We can learn more about these indicators and how they relate to us by taking a broader view.

NATURE VS. NURTURE

Our personality traits are part of a long-running debate over "Nature vs. Nurture" among developmental scientists trying to sort out how much of who we are is hard-set (natural) versus learned or environmental (nurtured).

Most experts agree this conflict includes more than a few "gray areas" and that personality traits are ultimately somewhat fluid. This is one good reason to avoid "typecasting" and it is why our study of personal convergence includes personality traits as just one of seven important background factors to assess.

Personality tests, surveys, assessments and profiles have long been used to help us learn how we're wired, how we can get along with others and how to find our best fits within organizations, career fields, etc. Two of the more popular profiles are the Myers-Briggs test and the DISC personality assessment.

The **Myers-Briggs Personality Test** is based on Carl Jung's famous book from 1921, Psychological Types. The Myers-Briggs Type Indicator assessment was developed by Katharine Cook Briggs and Isabel Briggs Myers during World War II for a consulting firm that Myers was working for. The assessment was designed to help women entering the workforce without prior experience, to seek the most compatible jobs.

The Myers-Briggs system is based on assessing a person's strongest natural preferences between opposite behavioral types.

These opposite types are broken into the following pairs (simplified here), based on each person's answers to a battery of questions:

E / I (Extroversion vs. Introversion) Are you energized around others or alone?

S / N (Sensing vs. Intuitive) Do you prefer concrete or intuitive conclusions?

T / F (Thinking vs. Feeling) Do you prefer logic or perception?

J / P (Judging vs. Perceiving) Do you like things structured or flexible?

John Gittinger developed the Personality Assessment System based on the Myers-Briggs model and identified 512 different "types" resulting from the combination of preferences to produce a personal profile such as E-S-T-J. This paradigm would help job seekers and their advisors locate the best "fit" for them. While some have argued that the numerous types can be confusing, the Meyers-Briggs test is still popular.

The most important takeaway from this system is that your personality is quite complex and that your preferences range from weak to strong in each area of measurement and that most people have certain traits that are dominant.

The DISC Assessment Tool is based on the DISC theory of psychologist William Marsten, a lawyer and psychologist who wrote Emotions of Normal People in 1928 and later produced the first lie-detector polygraph machine. He also wrote self-help books and created the Wonder Woman comic, based scandalously on his openly acknowledged mistress.

Marsten's theory identified four primary personality traits: Dominance, Inducement, Submission and Compliance. His theory was then developed into a personality test by industrial psychologist Walter Vernon Clarke and was modified later by John Geier for better and more concise results.

The assessment classifies four aspects of behavior by testing a person's preferences in word associations and are commonly used for screening job applicants, for educational purposes and for leadership assessment.

DISC is an acronym for:

> **Dominance or Drive** – relating to control, power and assertiveness.

Inducement or Influence – relating to social situations and communication.

Submission or Steadiness – relating to patience, persistence or thoughtfulness.

Compliance or Caution – relating to structure, organization and rules.

The DISC test aims to simplify matters by measuring your relative level in each category, so you can easily assess yourself as a "mid D, high I, mid S and low C," for example.

Given the thrust of these personality profiles, what can we surmise about David's personality traits? Would he have been an "I-S-F-J" on the Myers-Briggs, or perhaps a "high D, high I, low S and mid C" on the DISC? Without knowing more about David or about how he would select his preferences, we can only observe his actions and reach our own (speculative) conclusions.

But regardless of David's hypothetical personality profile, his personality traits were essential elements that converged with other key elements to produce his epic performance.

YOUR TRAITS AND MINE

As I review these traits, I'm reminded how much they impact our relationships, both personal and professional.

My marriage, for example, is almost comically built on opposite personality traits. I'm a night owl, my wife is an early bird. I'm an extrovert and she's an introvert, meaning I am energized by social engagements and activities while she is exhausted by them and needs hours if not days to recover, even after charming everyone with her enthusiasm, grace and humor when she participates. We thank God for our proverbial opposites-attract "chemistry," but the demands are very real.

Because she is also a "high S, high C" person, meaning she is very steady and compliant, while I am low in both respects, we can bump heads over things like my sometimes "creative" parking spots in unmarked or unusual areas (as opposed to her inside-the-lines compliance) or my spontaneous or innovative adventures.

These differences may seem minor if not trivial, but they call for serious respect for each other's traits and tendencies...or else. This is especially true in our case because we're also both "high D" assertive. So, consider yourself warned about these traits affecting your relationships!

Professionally, it is also important to recognize co-workers' (including bosses, partners and subordinates) personality traits and to adjust to them as appropriate. Where your traits align, you can celebrate and reinforce that "vibe" while trying to respect and carefully navigate your differences. Where there is no overlap or compensating "chemistry," you will have to try a little harder to get along.

In my business partnerships, I have been cognizant of both shared traits and different ones, usually with admiration and respect for my partners' different strengths, knowing they are valuable and even crucial to our success.

I would probably shy away from partnering with a "carbon copy" person who shares my same traits, for fear of duplication, overlap or role confusion, or to work with a "total opposite," although the latter would depend on chemistry and balance.

I make that proviso knowing that one of my best friends and closest associates (and biggest opposites), Craig Vogel, helps me with all my projects, and that Apple's co-founders Jobs and Wozniak did okay with that same pattern – at least for a while.

The takeaway here is that the better you know your own personality, the better you can seek the right role, job, career, mission or situation in life – and protect yourself (and others!) from situations that go against your grain.

GRIT, GUTS & GUMPTION

A final type of personality trait that doesn't appear on personality tests or assessments, and doesn't fit neatly into one of the other key areas of our overall study, is an intangible "X-factor" or mystery trait we might call fortitude, or what I've labeled above as grit, guts and gumption.

The Oxford definition of "fortitude" is simply "courage in pain or adversity.'

Definitions for my less formal words are similar, reflecting the attributes of courage, bravery, determination and resourcefulness.

Is there a "bravery" gene that we can inherit as part of our family history? Or is courage formed through our personal experiences or received as some kind of divine "gift" we receive by grace? If so, we could easily discuss this topic in other chapters.

We'll leave it here for now and consider it to be some kind of hard-wired, baked-in personality trait showcased by David for all the world to see and aspire to – but we'll keep it in mind as we continue.

And this reminds me of a friend who just happened to be one of my passengers in the car I crashed into the house, back in Chapter One. His name is Steve Islava and he has this bravery gene from what I can tell. I saw it in him when we were young, during a variety of high-stress situations, and therefore wasn't surprised when he became a longtime firefighter and paramedic.

Then, as if bravely facing terrible accident scenes and injuries wasn't enough, he had the *gumption* to invent life-saving medical products and equipment that have been widely adopted across the industry. That's some pretty cool convergence right there, and I've enjoyed witnessing it over the years.

I may not possess the same kind of life-saving bravery that first responders do, and I have found myself almost paralyzed by fear (like the solders facing Goliath) when facing certain high-pressure situations. But I have noticed a heroic trait that kicks in to conquer those fears, that we might call guts, and I recall how it helped me stand up to schoolyard bullies as a kid, and to confront a real-life (and very scary) beach bully I'll tell you about in an upcoming chapter.

So, please explore, claim and understand your personality traits and keep them in mind as we turn the page to explore the exciting topic of our gifts, talents and skills.

CHAPTER NINETEEN:

KEY #3: YOUR GIFTS, TALENTS & SKILLS

D avid was gifted, talented and skilled – and chances are you are, too.

These terms are often used interchangeably and there can certainly be some overlap between them. Collectively, these terms amount to what we might normally call our "abilities." But there are several distinctions worth noting to help you assess your gifts, talents and skills and harness them for maximum impact.

We'll explore each one while studying their implications for David, you and me.

GIFTS FROM ABOVE

A gifted person is naturally endowed with a special quality – the ancient Greek word for gift being *"charism"* (meaning grace) which is where we get the word charisma, which is another one of those elusive and intangible qualities to define, although the Oxford Dictionary tries with *"a divinely conferred power or talent."* When it comes to charisma, you simply know it when you see it.

As natural endowments, we cannot earn, buy, deserve or create our gifts, we can only embrace and employ them. Gifts can be physical beauty, unusual size, speed or qualities like high IQ, a photographic memory, extraordinary artistic or leadership ability. Mozart and Beethoven were gifted "pitch-perfect" composers (who could literally transcribe music that they heard), as are present or recent singers Celine Dion, Mariah Carey, Whitney Houston, Stevie Wonder, Michael Jackson and Brian Wilson.

Nikola Tesla, the world-famous inventor and electrical engineer, was gifted with a photographic memory, as were U.S. Presidents Teddy Roosevelt and Bill Clinton, author C.S. Lewis and Renaissance artist, architect and inventor Leonardo da Vinci.

Meanwhile, world record-holding sprinter Usain Bolt is a supremely gifted athlete as is current 7'4" basketball phenom, Victor Wembanyama. LeBron James is both physically and mentally gifted, with legendary size and strength along with an almost photographic memory of every player's position and activities on the floor of each game.

Ancient queen Esther's gift of beauty had brought her to the palace halls of power, after winning a nationwide beauty contest, where she could influence the king and save her people from genocide. Oprah Winfrey's charisma had similarly launched her from poverty to beauty pageant success to media opportunities and historic impact.

So, what was David's gift?

When he arrived on the battlefront to re-supply his brothers and wound up facing Goliath, he arrived with a hidden gift or "anointing" for leadership.

David's gift had been revealed during an earlier visit from Israel's leading prophet Samuel, who had traveled to David's family farm. Samuel was on a mission to anoint the next king of

Israel (to replace King Saul) from among the sons of Jesse, and he assumed the chosen one was the impressive eldest son, Eliab. He certainly looked the part.

But Samuel was stopped in his tracks, and prompted to keep looking.

Samuel inspected each of the handsome, leadership-worthy sons but could not confirm any of them as "the one." Frustrated, Samuel finally asked their father, Jesse, if he had any other sons to consider.

There was only one, of course, his youngest son David, and he was out shepherding in the fields. Once summoned, Samuel saw and confirmed David's anointing, and the rest is history.

This may explain Eliab's harsh reaction to David at the battlefront.

THE MEASURE OF OUR GIFTS

David's leadership gift would prove to be world-class and historic, as would his talent for song writing (most of the Psalms) and for architectural design (the temple built by his son Solomon in Jerusalem).

So where does that leave us?

Obviously, world-class or "all-time greatest" gifts are rare. But there are still plenty of gifts to go around.

Just think about the special gift, ability or quality you have received effortlessly, that requires nothing from you other than to steward, share or direct it. It could be your high IQ or your compassion, your natural strength, patience or sense of humor.

Whatever your gift, it's usually obvious and confirmed by others.

I've always felt gifted to communicate, encourage and inspire others, usually as a team or group leader. This ability was confirmed one night a number of years ago while attending a church leadership conference, while visiting friends in Arizona.

Right in the middle of a musical session, the guest speaker dialed the band's volume down and surveyed the crowd of several hundred people, as if searching for someone he knew – then stared and pointed directly at me sitting in the back (causing me to literally turn and look behind me for a second) and started speaking boldly like a prophet, saying God had given me a special ability to spark vision and faith in the hearts of people.

I felt like David plucked out from among his brothers for a special task, and have watched in faith ever since to see amazing things unfold, even as I sit and write this book. Time will tell the full measure of my gift, how far it will reach and how many it will touch. But right now, I'm thankful it has allowed me to reach you.

As we steward our gifts and direct our talents, we learn more about their measure – just as I did when I played pro football.

As you might recall, I wasn't an especially gifted athlete, but I was still talented and determined enough to play a few years and ultimately sign with a Super Bowl champion team.

That was as far as I could go with my measure of grace – as opposed to a truly gifted high school opponent of mine from Santa Monica High School named Dennis Smith. Smith was a 6'3" 200lb. safety and receiver who set a California state high jump record of 6'10" as just a teenager, then went on to an All-American football career at USC and an All-Pro career with the Denver Broncos, complete with three Super Bowl appearances.

Yes, I was determined, but Dennis Smith was truly gifted and determined.

Gaining a realistic assessment of our gifts, talents and skills becomes essential to establishing reasonable goals and expectations – and to enjoying the greatest amount of happiness and contentment as we seek to meet or exceed them.

Are you gifted? If so, your special ability has probably been recognized and affirmed many times, in many ways – hopefully by trusted (or divinely appointed!) messengers.

Do you know what level or measure of gifting you have? The greater your gift the larger the role it will likely play in your personal convergence.

If you don't have a "big" or obvious gift, don't despair. We all have talents and skills to fill the gap.

CULTIVATE & EXERCISE YOUR TALENTS

A talented person has a special ability to do something well. Much like gifts, talents are naturally endowed and need to be embraced and employed. But talents tend to be more specialized than gifts, for example a "talent for math" is different than a genius level IQ. A "talented violinist" is different than a musical genius.

Gifts are a given, whether exercised or utilized or not. Talents are more action oriented and are revealed through activity.

Thankfully our world is full of talented people, whether they be mechanics, carpenters, teachers, engineers, doctors and scientists, musicians, athletes, artists or any number of others.

David was a talented communicator, as evidenced by his speech to King Saul, his defiant words to Goliath and years later, the many Psalms that he wrote.

David was also a talented musician (harp player), shepherd and warrior, able to perform soothing songs for a fitful king, fight off a lion and bear, and drop a giant with his deadly accurate sling.

My best talents (besides washing the car or leaf-blowing the yard!) have always been writing and speaking, followed by coaching, advising or teaching.

What are your talents? How are they employed? Is there one that is most outstanding? Fortunately, talents lend themselves to cultivation, development and specialization, and frequently morph into well-honed skills.

HONE YOUR SKILLS

A skilled person has the training, knowledge or experience to do something well. Skills are often needed to take raw talent to the "next level" and produce maximum impact. The naturally gifted or talented athlete must train to develop skills by learning and practicing proper techniques. The same thing applies to an artist or a techie.

David presumably honed his skills with a sling through countless hours of practice in the fields while shepherding. We can imagine him conquering boredom by slinging stones day after day, year after year, hitting one target after another.

The talented "numbers person" must still learn accounting principles, tax law and much more to realize his or her full potential as a financial advisor. Even a talented surgeon needs to develop surgical skills and add medical knowledge – not just rely on natural talent or intelligence.

No matter how gifted or talented a person might be, skills will usually determine their ultimate impact. Without David's skillful use of his sling, we wouldn't even know his name, let alone his family background, personality traits or dramatic life story.

Thankfully, most of us can develop productive and marketable skills through education and/or training, no matter how much gifting or talent we possess. And if our skills align with our family history, dreams or personality traits, so much the better!

David's skill with a sling was his "secret weapon" to defeat Goliath.

What are your most developed skills? Which of your skills are most marketable? Which are most aligned with your talents, interests and personality traits? Are there skills you need to develop to fully utilize your talents or to reach your "next level" and achieve maximum impact?

Gifts, talents and skills are critical components to achieving personal convergence. So take some time to contemplate the questions above. Jot down some notes. Ask your family members or friends (or relevant professionals) for honest feedback about your gifting, talents and skills.

Start thinking about how you can cultivate, hone and employ your abilities to realize your ultimate visions, dreams and passions.

Because that's where we're going next!

CHAPTER TWENTY:

KEY #4: YOUR VISIONS, DREAMS & PASSIONS

D avid was passionate about his God, family, tribe and nation. That passion ignited his heroic effort to defend them against Goliath and the Philistines.

David was also passionate about songs, music and worship. After he became king of Israel at the age of 30, he arranged for musicians and singers to perform worship 24/7 in their capital city of Jerusalem. His passion for music and song also infused the many Psalms he wrote to worship God and encourage his people.

David possessed a vision and a dream, as well.

He dreamed of building a beautiful temple in Jerusalem where his God could be worshipped with appropriate awe and splendor. And though he wasn't allowed to build the temple himself (being disqualified as a man of war), his dream begat the clear vision he expressed through his architectural plans and extensive efforts to collect funds, workers and materials for his son Solomon to construct the temple.

David's dreams, visions and passions marked history and continue to touch millions of people throughout the world.

How about you and yours? Let's break them down for fresh perspective.

DREAMS & VISIONS TO DIE FOR

Inspired dreams that imagine a better world and refuse to die are the stuff of legend. History's greatest example may be Martin Luther King Jr.'s vivid and compelling "I have a dream" speech of August 28, 1963, delivered on the steps of the Lincoln Memorial in Washington, DC.

This speech was written for a special event promoting civil rights legislation proposed by President John F. Kennedy. It also paid homage to Abraham Lincoln's Gettysburg Address and corresponded with the 100-year centennial of the Emancipation Proclamation.

This historic event represented quite a convergence in it's own right. But there was a bigger one coming.

Though MLK was one of 18 speakers to address the crowd that day, his words stand alone and continue to soar and inspire millions of people today.

Why such impact?

King was a naturally gifted, renowned and charismatic leader from a family line of gifted leaders and talented preachers, including his father who changed MLK's name for inspirational purposes, as we learned three chapters ago.

He was a highly skilled communicator who labored to write and perfect his messages with colorful, compelling and dramatic words of life, truth and hope.

As a leading civil rights activist and the first president of the Southern Christian Leadership Conference, he was a proven and well-positioned leader whose message was authenticated by his dedication to his cause – fully aware that he was risking death in the process.

Undeterred by fear, MLK's personal convergence was on full display that day.

Besides harnessing and directing every part of his personal history, dreams and DNA for his task, Dr. King did what every successful dreamer must do – he found a way to share his dream in a clear, colorful and concrete way. He wrote it down, reworked it a number of times and finally spoke it out loud in its final and dramatic form.

King presented his dream and exhorted others to share it with him – and his dream continues to inspire social, spiritual and political transformation, sixty years later. We will discuss why his dream is a model for ours today, as we proceed.

Another visionary who left an indelible mark on history was Joan of Arc.

Joan of Arc was the 17-year-old peasant girl who became France's patron saint after receiving heavenly visions of battlefield success during France's 100 Years War against England's invasion of France, in 1429.

The insistent teenager demanded an audience with her nation's leaders and soon led them – most dramatically on horseback sprinting into battle, wearing armor and sword and flying her famous banner – toward battles that successfully regained strategic cities and territories, including the place where France's uncrowned King Charles could enjoy a proper coronation.

Like Martin Luther King Jr. and so many noble heroes over the years, Joan of Arc was willing to die for her cause. Tragically, she was wounded in battle, then captured and killed a couple of years later.

A REAL (ABNORMAL) DREAM

When it comes to "normal" dreams (i.e., while sleeping), some people clearly remember them and can even interpret them after waking up. But I normally don't and can't. My recollections are usually foggy and fleeting at best, by the time I wake up.

Except for the dream that redirected my life in the fall of 1999.

My season of full-time ministry had run its course, and I was transitioning back to regular work, managing fleet sales of trucks and SUVs at a local Ford dealership while seeking my next opportunity. Then I woke up from a dream.

In that crystal clear dream, I was brainstorming with my old friend and sports media partner, Andy Bark, working together on a whiteboard, excitedly diagramming business strategies like football X's and O's.

The strange thing was I hadn't seen or spoken to Andy for a few years, so I was reluctant to contact him "out of the blue." But finally, I picked up the phone and gave him a call.

When I told him about my dream and laughed about needing a strange reason to call and catch up, he listened but didn't laugh. After a moment he said, "Dude, we need to talk. You would not believe what's going on with us right now."

He proceeded to explain how he had battled to save the company after I had left and then again when he had clashed with the investor himself, and had almost lost the company. But he had managed to salvage enough of it to survive and then expand nationwide, now as Student Sports Inc. He had created and produced Football Training camps with and for Nike all across the country, had developed Elite 11 Quarterback camps and had even won Emmy Awards working with Fox Sports.

Now he had venture capital groups as well as Fox Sports Net offering major investment and partnership deals to further expand the company. "I could really use your help," he said. So we agreed to meet and talk.

Within weeks we were strategizing and negotiating a multimillion dollar partnership with Fox Sports Net, complete with notes and diagrams on the whiteboard. I was soon negotiating a lease for modern glass-paneled office spaces overlooking Torrance Airport and heading up our sales and marketing division as Executive Vice President, working on deals with national players like Procter & Gamble, EA Sports, 24 Hour Fitness and The Sporting News.

I was happier than a pig in slop!

An unusual dream had returned me to my dream job and venture, allowing me to realize the long-lost vision for our company's national expansion ten years later. This supernatural turn of events also reinforced my belief in the invisible yet obvious forces at work in, through and around our visions, dreams and passions.

IMAGINE WHAT'S POSSIBLE

Walt Disney once said, "Vision is our ability to see the future with imagination." Hopefully you will re-read that profound nugget and then borrow, steal, recite, share and memorize it the way I have, because it offers a life-changing perspective that echoes the wisdom of history's greatest "possibility thinkers."

Disney didn't start with an entertainment empire. In fact, his first venture, Laugh-O-Gram Studio went bankrupt after its semi-popular cartoon strips failed to pay the rent.

But Disney continued to envision a kingdom full of imaginary characters and experiences based on his years of sketching, studying, animating and producing, starting with a character named Mickey Mouse, reportedly based on a little mouse who kept him company in his low-rent office.

Disney originally named his cartoon character Mortimer Mouse, but his wife Lillian suggested Mickey was catchier and "less pompous." This is a great reminder that even visionaries need helpful advice, counsel or feedback every once in a while.

Disney soon followed Mickey Mouse with Snow White, Pinocchio, Dumbo, Bambi, Cinderella, Sleeping Beauty, Mary Poppins and a groundbreaking new theme park called Disneyland, in Southern California.

Meanwhile, President John F. Kennedy's "moon-shot" vision for sending astronauts to the moon required almost unimaginable imagination!

In Kennedy's epic "We choose to go to the Moon" speech on September 12, 1962, he spoke of a new frontier and called upon America's pioneering spirit and technological talent to create the plans, set the goals and do the work to make it happen as quickly as possible. He spoke with urgency and passion.

More recently, in the midst of the economic turmoil of America's Great Recession of 2008, Elon Musk took the CEO position at Tesla Inc., after buying a majority stake in the company and leading much of its private funding and design work over several years.

A couple years later, on June 29th, 2010, Musk showcased his company's stylish, battery-powered Tesla Roadster to the world as his company launched its stock to the general public on Wall Street. It was the first American car company IPO since The Ford Motor Company's offering in 1956, and it launched what became one of the world's most valuable companies.

Tesla stock sold for just $17 a share that day and it has split twice and climbed many times higher since.

Just as Musk had imagined futuristic cars and space travel as a child, drawing pictures of rockets and space vehicles, he could imagine the public's positive reception to well-designed electric cars before anyone else could – with the same kind of imagination that formed and launched his space-travel company, Space-X.

Even my teenage hero, Arnold Schwarzenegger, is a role model for vision-casting, dreams and imagination. As a teenager in Austria, Arnold posted pictures of the world's greatest body-builders on his wall and vividly imagined himself in their position, winning trophies and championships all around the world, then passionately worked to make it happen.

He later imagined himself starring in Hollywood movies and took humble yet determined steps in that direction, even though his heavy German accent and unusual profession seemed to disqualify him as a misfit.

Today I tell people that "vision is contagious" because Arnold's realized vision later inspired my own, to build my skinny body into something bigger, stronger and more capable of realizing my dream of playing pro football. And I have seen other forms of vision "rub off" on me and many others, along the way.

NUTS, BOLTS & PASSIONS

Are you captive to a dream or vision? Are you fueled by a particular passion?

If so, have you written it down, posted a picture, sketched a plan or broken it down into concrete terms? Have you organized your thoughts and shared your dreams with others, or have you hidden them away for fear of ridicule or failure?

It's time to consider the nuts and bolts of chasing your dream, realizing your vision or fulfilling your passion.

Yes, visions, dreams and passions require nuts and bolts.

Being passionate about something without a clear action plan is a recipe for disaster, frustration and disillusionment.

If you're passionate about building skyscrapers, you better have blueprints. If you're passionate about improving your fitness, you better have a diet and workout plan. If you're passionate about a new business venture, you better create a business plan.

David's passion for building a temple led him to create detailed designs and building plans. MLK's passion for equality shaped not just his speeches and sermons but the social programs and political reforms he crafted or promoted.

Passion without plans or structure can lead to chaos and disapointment.

When you translate your visions, dreams or passions into plans, I suggest you follow this simple outline and approach:

1. **Your destination, goal or target.** Make it big, clear and compelling. Picture it. It should energize and magnetize you – drawing you toward it every day.

2. **Your phases, stages and steps.** Break it down into simple and measurable steps, portions and timeframes. You want steady progress and momentum.

3. **Your day, week and month.** Make sure you know and complete your top 3 priorities for each day, week and month. All the rest are secondary and will follow the top three.

LIKE A BRICK HOUSE

I put this approach to the test, recently, on a renovation project we completed on a 50-year-old brick house at Cedar Creek Lake, near Dallas, TX.

I decided to act as our general contractor due to the home's distance from our usual contractors, and because I wanted to control all aspects of this super personal "passion project."

The experience (and result) was fantastic, starting with the clear and compelling vision we had to transform the drab and dated property into a striking Nantucket blue home with white trim, a yellow door, new windows, gutters, a second deck, rails on the dock, white picket fencing and a total designer-style makeover inside.

Despite the typical weather, subcontractor and product delays, each phase, project and coordinated step of the process came together as I focused on the daily, weekly and monthly priorities noted above. Following that outline and working together with our team, we were able to make our dream come true, and so can you as you follow the same blueprint.

You can see the house @nicholas4success (under Properties+) on Instagram if you're interested.

PASSION POWER

The good news about passion is that once it's properly harnessed and directed, it becomes your ultimate X-factor for success.

As my college linebacker coach used to say, "Nothing great was ever accomplished without enthusiasm." His enthusiasm was so contagious it helped both me and my linebacking partner, John Woodring, rise and shine enough to gain notice, earn contracts and play professionally (him with the New York Jets), in spite of our small college status.

No, nothing great, new or different happens without some horsepower, willpower, "juice" or "fire in the belly" behind it. Passion means *"full of intense emotion,"* while the word "enthusiasm" means *"full of God's spirit"* in the ancient Greek language.

David was passionate enough to stand up to a deadly warrior who had paralyzed an army. MLK was passionate enough to speak up to centuries of injustice. I was passionate enough to study and train to turn my disastrous life around.

History is full of epic success stories fueled, stoked and inflamed by passion. What is yours?

If your passion is fully ablaze, then God bless you – let it propel you forward. If you find yourself a little lukewarm in the passion department, don't be discouraged. Even David once wrote that he had to command his spirit to rise up, and maybe you have to do the same. You must stir up the embers of your hopes and dreams. You can pray for heavenly fire and direction. You can generate some passion and slay the Goliath in your life or build something wonderful.

Now let's explore how our personal experiences – both positive and negative – can help us target and achieve epic lives.

CHAPTER TWENTY-ONE:

KEY #5: YOUR PERSONAL EXPERIENCES

David came from the right time and place to battle Goliath. He possessed the right traits, talents, dreams and passions, too. But he needed something more.

He needed permission from the king.

Like a zealous young entrepreneur seeking financial backing from an investor, or a low-ranking staff member pitching a bold new program to his or her department head, David was putting his leader at serious risk – and on the spot.

Even the most hopeful and supportive investor, supervisor or king is afraid of the embarrassing blowback that can follow their premature approval or promotion of young or ambitious talent. And King Saul was right there, as the determined teenager David was making his case. "Let me at him," David was basically saying, "I can take that guy!"

It was pretty hard to believe his pitch – and even harder to endorse it. It was much easier to imagine David's terrible death at the hands of the ferocious giant, right in front of Saul's entire army.

Until David mentioned the lion and the bear.

"I have killed both a lion and a bear while guarding our sheep," said David. "So I can definitely take that ugly chump standing over there," he added confidently, in so many words.

This is what HR professionals call "relatable experience." And it often leads to the hiring manager saying, "Please, tell me more!"

In David's case, his rare experience was enough to earn the king's blessing.

GOOD, BAD & UGLY

David's confidence may have also come from his experience being singled out and anointed to be the next King of Israel by Samuel the prophet, which we discussed earlier as one of his gifts.

He may have even been motivated to take center stage, in front of his nation's whole army, to demonstrate the leadership he felt stirring within him.

Like everyone, however, David's life would include a mixture of good, bad and ugly experiences as it unfolded over the years – including his responsibility for the death of Bathsheba's husband, after his infamous adultery with her.

Despite that great failure (or maybe because of it), David was able to learn from his mistakes, turn himself around and maintain a positive attitude and posture toward the challenges, betrayals, hostilities and other bad experiences he encountered.

Positive experiences can naturally influence our direction in life and reinforce our efforts or behavior that led to them. They can generate momentum we can foster, cultivate and build upon. This is like athletes or teams "stacking wins," and is something we'll revisit in a moment.

Our greatest challenge, though, is to address and overcome bad or ugly experiences. To learn from them and turn them around for redemptive purposes.

This is how John Newton, the one-time slave trader and author of *Amazing Grace* overcame his ugly experiences, including his abuse as a cabin boy pressed into the British navy, and then as an abusive slave ship captain. Miraculously, he was able to reverse his course and experience redemption, both spiritually and politically.

In fact, Newton's personal influence upon a young William Wilberforce led to Wilberforce's tireless and almost singlehanded campaign in Britain's Parliament to banish slave trading in all British territories, beginning in 1807, almost 60 years before it happened in America.

This is similar to the challenge faced and overcome by Oprah Winfrey and so many other victims of emotional, racial or sexual abuse. They have rallied to face their terrible experiences and have refused to be shackled or defined by them, usually through the power of forgiveness and recovery, and through their efforts to educate and empower others.

Addressing our negative experiences and converting them into redemptive ones should be among our greatest goals and aspirations.

REVISIT YOUR VICTORIES

As I have interviewed and talked casually with fellow athletes, I have noticed something very interesting. When you ask them about their most memorable wins and losses, it's amazing how quickly they cut to their most vivid and painful *losses*, personal *failures* and last-minute *defeats!* Their feel-good wins somehow blur together into pleasant memories, while the heartbreaking losses create unforgettable scars.

Of all my memories, for instance, the most vivid and intense is the scrambling quarterback who got away to throw a last-minute touchdown pass to beat my high school team in our championship game – just minutes after I caught a touchdown pass to put us ahead.

That QB literally slipped out of my arms during a sack that would have ended the game right where we landed. Instead, a teammate accidentally knocked me off the determined scrambler when he dove to help me take him down, freeing the QB to extend the winning play.

Adding to the pain was a promise I made during a timeout right before that play, that if our coach sent me on a linebacker blitz, I would get that dang quarterback.

So that one still stings.

In glowing contrast, David reminds us why we need to remember, revisit and recite our victories.

We all know that confidence and success go hand in hand, each supporting and enhancing the other. So anything we can do to increase our confidence – without becoming *overconfident* – is extremely valuable and important to ourselves and to others around us.

Why? Because confidence is contagious.

Formula One racecar driver Max Verstappen burst onto the racing scene at an early age, much the way David did on the battlefield. He was bursting with confidence.

And his reason was similar, since he had proven himself racing at every level since he was a young boy.

He had killed both lion and bear. And now, today, he dominates the entire sport.

MY REAL-LIFE BEACH BULLY

In one of my Instagram videos, I revisit the site of a hallmark experience in my life that speaks to this whole subject of confidence-building.

One summer, when I was 12 years old, I felt nervous every morning.

I wasn't nervous about the beach runs, buoy swims or other challenges my friends and I endured as part of the Junior Lifeguards beach program we attended.

I was scared to death of the bully in our group.

This kid was big, strong, looked 16, hung around with "burnouts" (older surfer-dude stoners), had a couple of big buddies by his side and he hated me and my friends as members of a rival town.

He pushed kids around, "borrowed" our surfboards (and sometimes stomped them on the sand), constantly threatening physical harm to anyone who resisted.

I tried to steer clear of him…until something happened one morning.

It was during our daily wet-sand beach run to the rocky cliffs a quarter mile away and back. I was toward the front of the pack returning from the cliffs when I heard voices yelling from the stragglers behind us and turned around to see a shocking site.

With other kids watching in fear, the bully had pinned one of our smallest friends under his knees along the water line and was sitting on him holding a jellyfish high above his head, with its dangerous tentacles dangling down close to his face!

I grabbed my friend Brant Blakeman, stopped and pointed. "Let's go!" I said, he nodded, and we sprinted toward the scene.

We arrived with a bang! We sent the bully sprawling as we knocked him off our friend. The bully gathered himself quickly, ferociously, and was now suddenly on the attack.

We quickly retreated and split as the bully came charging after us. He then decided to chase *me*, probably because I looked weaker than my husky friend Brant.

(He didn't know I had taken down playground bullies in the past after moving to new schools as "the new kid," or had been toughened up by older brothers.)

But he was both furious and dangerous, so I backpedaled up the slope of the beach to where I stood a bit higher, as he slowed to calculate his attack.

I then planted myself with fists up, ready.

He lunged toward me, swinging wildly, as I retreated, then dodged and danced around like Muhammad Ali, suddenly filled with adrenaline-packed swagger. I flicked several jabs, started talking a little trash, and then landed a hard right to his nose that ended the fight.

He hurried away with a bloody nose, some tears in his eyes and his buddies escorting him to wherever beach bullies go.

The celebration was short-lived, however, because I was scared to death he'd come back with his dangerous older friends to get me.

Thankfully, when he returned the next week, he was a different kid.

And so was I.

When the summer program ended and awards were handed, out I wasn't expecting to win anything. I was never our fastest runner, swimmer or top event winner.

But apparently, by a vote of my peers, I was our Most Valuable Junior Lifeguard. Even got the plaque to prove it.

MARKER EVENTS

I have re-visited this experience many times over the years, and I still cherish the award, for so many reasons. It's funny how make-believe it seems sometimes now, like a movie about someone else.

And yet it's all very real, like the other real-life victories I have learned to revisit. Whether it's to rebuild my confidence after facing traumatic setbacks (like my car crash or business failures) or to muster confidence for tackling new projects or challenges or even simply to marvel at life and further boost my spirits when things are going well.

The beach bully was one of my lions or bears.

What are yours?

To give you an idea, I can think of plenty possible candidates from my family members' victories alone. My daughter's poetry reading championships in grade school or her graduation from Chicago Law School. One son's spelling bee victory in middle school, wrestling medals in high school or his fast-track rise to directorship at his insurance firm.

I remember my other son's 6th grade victory as class president, after overcoming his extreme shyness to deliver a funny election speech, and his determination to win BMX bike races, and my wife's epic mid-life detour to study, pass tests and become a beloved "rockstar" teacher at a Title I elementary school in Watts, and then at another one later, in McKinney, TX.

Bravery, courage, determination and success. All good things to celebrate.

Yes, we naturally recall – and often *dwell* – on our most painful experiences. So recalling, revisiting and reciting your victories might feel awkward or selfish or even ridiculous to you. But take it from David and me. Try it and see.

In the process, let's explore how to recognize and embrace our seasons.

CHAPTER TWENTY-TWO:

KEY #6: YOUR SEASONS, SETBACKS & PREPARATION

Shepherding sheep was not exactly glamorous work, even back in ancient times when life was hard for everyone.

Shepherds were considered "low-end' laborers, even then.

David was presumably stuck with the job because his older brothers didn't want to do it. Such is life when you're the entry level employee, the low person on the org chart or the youngest member of the family business.

Sometimes you get stuck with the stinky, lonely or mindless jobs and have to prove your worth before graduating from that position, level or season to the next.

Apparently, David made the most of his "entry level" season by using the time to write songs, play music and sharpen his rock-slinging skills – all things that would become central to his life and success, later.

This alone is a worthy reminder to make the very most of every season. But David gives us more.

After he defeated Goliath, David became a popular hero and a growing leadership threat to King Saul. This forced David to endure a difficult season of waiting and survival, as the jealous king chased and hunted to kill him for some time. David insisted on waiting for his proper time to become king, however.

Even when David had Saul "dead to rights" and within easy reach to kill him on more than one occasion, he could not justify murder, and chose to wait. He trusted Gods laws, favor and timing instead of his own, probably mindful that we usually "reap what we sow."

Ultimately, David's season of waiting paid off and he became king – strengthened by the maturity, wisdom and leadership ability he gained in the process.

What looked like setbacks to David's ultimate success – being stuck in the fields tending sheep or later surviving in the wilderness while on the run – would ultimately become essential to his legacy and success.

A TIME FOR EVERYTHING

In the ancient book of Ecclesiastes we read, "There is a time for everything, and for everything under heaven there is a season."

The passage proceeds with a long list of simple yet profound things ranging from a time to be born and a time to die, to a time to mourn and a time to dance.

This passage reminds us how we need to recognize and embrace the times and seasons we encounter, to make the most of them and to prepare for them.

Even as I write this chapter here in Dallas, Texas, the weather outside has suddenly changed from months of 100-degree temperatures to almost freezing, thus offering a brisk reminder that I can't keep wearing swim trunks and T-shirts! My wife always looks ahead and prepares, while I am sometimes slow to adjust.

Just as calendar seasons change from summer to fall and winter to spring, and even sports seasons cycle from soccer and baseball to football, basketball and hockey each year, we encounter a variety of seasons, just as David did.

I'm reminded of Nelson Mandella, South Africa's revolutionary leader who endured 27 years of imprisonment – an almost eternal season of waiting, sowing and preparation – before his release to lead his country out of its racial bondage, and to reap a harvest. It was a season he had to endure and embrace and maximize to become the man of destiny he became.

I'm reminded of Oprah Winfrey's destiny for great and wonderful media success, who first embraced a humble season of local radio news reading, to showcase her talent, learn her craft and prepare for much bigger opportunities to come.

Even Steve Jobs, after being forced out of his own company at Apple, embraced that painful season and made the most of it, buying George Lucas' special effects company and turning it into the breakthrough animation company, Pixar, known for producing box office mega-hits including *Toy Story, Cars* and *The Incredibles.*

He later returned to reignite the fortunes of Apple, but his "season of exile" at Pixar demonstrates how even painful setbacks can create fruitful seasons of their own.

One more favorite example of mine is Dwayne "The Rock" Johnson, who has fully embraced and maximized his seasons and setbacks in pursuit of his dreams. Growing up in the "family business" of professional wrestling, he yearned to travel beyond it, first as a baller at the University of Miami and then in the pros. Unfortunately, his football dream died where mine gained life, when he was signed, asked to change positions and later released by the Calgary Stampeders in the CFL.

He embraced his setback, however, and chose to pursue his dreams through professional wrestling and then managed to travel beyond it, to occasional film and TV appearances and to his pivotal football dream-affirming cable series, *Ballers*. He's continued to move onward and upward with starring roles in blockbuster films and other creative projects and enjoys a social media following among the world's largest today.

NAVIGATING NEW SEASONS

If history teaches us anything about navigating new seasons, it's our need to *recognize* them, so we can properly adjust our trajectory – no matter how suddenly or unexpectedly they arrive.

As you might recall from my story in Chapter 15, when I was suddenly forced out of my sports media company, I soon embraced a "season of study" which led to a life-changing period of full-time ministry, serving as a pastor.

That season was easy to recognize, and it was joyful and exciting to pursue, even though we had to sell our home and move away from our families for a while to make it happen. That season had its challenges but it was definitely blessed and miraculous in many ways.

When the next season arrived more dramatically (through the dream that led me back to the sports media company in Chapter 20), it was also easy to recognize and navigate, and it represented a season of unparalleled personal convergence.

But then another season arrived like a hurricane, thanks to 9/11.

A month or so after the terrorist-driven planes hit the twin towers, I was standing at Ground Zero in the darkness of night, with the chilly fog blowing over from the Hudson River, thinking about my long day of discouraging meetings with sports media advertisers too scared to make commitments. I was watching the 24/7 work crews dig and pick through the massive mountains of rubble, under the eerie light of the construction site lamps, thinking about all the souls who perished there, and wondering about my own plight.

Our eventual parent company was a publicly traded NASDAQ firm that expected immediate and profitable results. Now the market was frozen in fear and uncertainty.

Tragically, it wouldn't take long for our sales figures to lag and for our parent company to start cutting budgets. And they would begin by cutting me.

I will tell you what happened next, as we explore the subject of your opportunities and challenges.

CHAPTER TWENTY-THREE:

KEY #7: YOUR OPPORTUNITIES & CHALLENGES

David's history-making opportunity came dressed up as a hair-raising, adrenaline pumping, life-threatening confrontation with a fiercely imposing enemy determined to chop him up and feed him to the buzzards.

Yes, the greatest opportunities often look like the worst kinds of challenges.

Just as "one man's trash is another man's treasure," one person's problem can be another person's opportunity. Everything depends on our perspective, on how we *see things*.

History is filled with leaders and heroes who simply saw things differently than others. Where others fixated on closed doorways they saw "windows of opportunity," often forced open by adversity.

Leaders and heroes arise in the midst of hardship and chaos, just as the brightest lights emerge from darkness. As explained in an earlier chapter, the Chinese symbol for "crisis" combines the symbols for both danger and opportunity – something David would have understood.

It has also been said that "luck" happens when preparation meets opportunity. Opportunities surround us every day – if we have the eyes to see them and the will to seize them. Our greatest challenge is to keep our eyes and spirits open to sometimes scary or even horrific opportunities.

A brave young English woman named Florence Nightingale saw the deadly and nightmarish conditions of battlefield care for wounded soldiers during the Crimean War of 1853-1856 and responded with innovative care that miraculously reversed their staggering death rates and gave birth to the modern nursing movement and the profession of nursing that we know, admire and respect today.

Florence had to fight her way through family opposition and cultural norms, just to be there, let alone to pioneer a whole new career field.

Another young woman named Mary Teresa Bojaxhiu became a nun and saw the misery, death and poverty around her in Calcutta, India. This is where people were literally dying in the streets, abandoned and alone.

Later known as Mother Teresa, the young woman founded a charitable movement that grew to involve over 4,500 nuns in 133 countries. Her missions offered dignity, hospice care and love to "the poorest of the poor," people she had chosen as her "target demographic." Millions of patients and volunteers were touched as a result.

SLIGHTLY LESS DRAMATIC

I know these stories are dramatic, if not extreme.

And I realize such epic stories can easily intimidate the rest of us mere mortals. My purpose for sharing them is not to intimidate but to share graphic examples we can easily remember and apply toward our lives and circumstances.

Thankfully, there are plenty of opportunities that don't come with such terrifying challenges attached. But they still may require significant leaps of faith to reach, seize and grab hold of them.

As you might recall, our previous chapter ended with the proverbial "axe" hanging over my neck, as the terrorist attacks of 9/11 disrupted the economy and froze the advertising industry, right when we needed ad sales to heat up for our company.

When that didn't happen, bad things happened to me.

I quickly went from being a happy high-flying six-figure sports media company co-founder to an unemployed, crashed, burned and broke dreamer in despair.

But I wasn't laying down having a pity party.

My eyes were open to the next season and opportunity, and I managed to find a great one – in Knoxville, Tennessee.

I had applied for the six-figure CEO position of Knoxville's flagship non-profit ministry serving the homeless and others in recovery programs downtown, with additional safe houses for battered and abused women from the community.

A professional executive search firm was handling their hiring process and that process dragged on for several months. There were in-depth applications, psychological tests, personality assessments, interviews and more interviews. I kept hearing positive feedback as they thinned their pool of prospects down to a final few, but the process continued as I remained in limbo.

They finally flew me out to meet and speak with their board of directors, then flew me out again, this time with my wife. They had thinned the field down to two.

Was this a bullseye job for me? Probably not, but it offered a new season to work hard, touch lives, make a positive impact and settle down.

Then they picked the other finalist.

I had put "all my eggs in one basket," and now I was in a real mess.

A CONVERGANT OPPORTUNITY

It was a cold, dark night, and I was driving just outside of Bakersfield, California., in the middle of nowhere.

That's how it felt anyway, as I drove home to Los Angeles, defeated and alone. After losing the Knoxville position, I had driven up to meet a former sports media client and friend in Bakersfield about possibly joining his company. But after meeting all afternoon we realized it wasn't going to work. It just wasn't the right fit.

Now Christmas was coming in a week, and I was heading home empty-handed, broke and in debt. Things were so tight I was watching my gas gauge and knew we couldn't afford a Christmas tree, let alone presents to put under it. I was embarrassed and depressed and had reached an all-time low point.

Then my cell phone rang.

It was a friend of mine named Dan Frank, calling out of the blue from Dallas. He wanted to know how I was doing.

"Not so well." I told him, before sharing more about my predicament.

He was calling to see if I might consider coming to Dallas to help him build his small but up-and-coming real estate company. So we discussed his business and the leadership role he envisioned for me, then agreed that he would fly me and my wife out to meet with him and his wife, tour the city and talk further – immediately. He wanted to move fast, and my situation was urgent, too.

I saw key elements converging in this prospective partnership, in my life and in my friend's background. As I surveyed my friend's natural gifts, talents, skills and personality traits, I recognized how well they fit the innovative company he was building with its unique array of boutique services for investors, corporate relocation, home builders, flips, online buyers and guaranteed buy-out programs for traditional home sellers. It was really brilliant and innovative stuff.

I also recognized a new season and rare opportunity at hand, and saw tremendous potential for my creative input, marketing savvy and work ethic to complement his. It was a huge opportunity.

But it wouldn't come easy. The challenge was pretty giant, too.

We would have to leave our hometown, move 1,500 miles and start over, at 40-plus years old with kids in school, in a very different part of the country. I would have to learn the business, get licensed, oversee marketing and finally test my longtime interest (and grandfather's legacy) in real estate to see if I could help build a small company into something bigger, and hopefully bless a bunch of future employees, agents, clients and my family as we grew.

Would the possible reward be worth the very real risks?

By the time we flew home from our Dallas meeting, we had a generous agreement in place, offering quick ownership interest, an immediate executive role and a starting bonus wired to our account before Christmas Day arrived.

Miraculously, there would be gifts under the tree.

I would drive to Dallas and start the day after New Year's and move my family there within six months, if everything went well.

HITTING YOUR TARGET

Things have gone well here for almost 20 years now. We built the small firm into the #1 sales team in Texas (and #2 in the US) within just three years and we were able to buy a beautiful old home with towering trees, a pool, high ceilings and stately custom touches within just 18 months – the first one we owned since selling our first place to pursue ministry, so many years ago.

I had discovered the home and its "For Sale by Owner" sign well before I had any prayer of buying a home, in a neighborhood called Eldorado named after the mythical "City of Gold" featuring fabulous wealth and opportunity that for centuries drew treasure-seekers to the jungles of South America.

I was still living with my friend and his family in Frisco, TX and was trying to find a home for my family to live in after finishing the school year back home and moving out to join me.

As soon as I saw the house, it reminded me of my grandfather's mansion in Chicago and spoke to my deepest desires. I called and befriended the owner and we negotiated a very special "friends and family" kind of lease/option to buy contract that allowed us to lease and live there immediately and buy it when we could.

I tell you about this home not to brag or to boast (yet again!), but to reinforce our conversation about opportunities and challenges, faith and imagination.

The opportunity in this case was an owner who wanted to sell his house privately to avoid commissions and control the process. The challenge was I couldn't afford it or qualify to buy it at that time.

So I explored the opportunity by faith, in search of a creative win-win solution to acquire the home, and got the owner to lease it to us until we could buy it, roughly a year later. You can see this home and hear more about the story behind it on the video I produced for my last book, at FreeDebtVideo.com.

There will always be turbulence in life, along with difficult seasons and challenging times that come and go.

The Great Recession of 2008 killed real estate for a while, for instance, and even shut down our magical real estate firm. But I opened a new firm of my own and have continued brokering properties and even added remodeling design and project management services, to my great enjoyment.

Challenges are usually tailor-made opportunities for someone, why not us?

The key is to see and assess them through the lens of personal convergence to ensure that they align with your history, dreams and DNA.

If you've been anointed as the next king of Israel, you've killed a lion and a bear, and you wield a wickedly accurate sling (and have a big chip on your shoulder with something to prove) then a king's reward for conquering Goliath looks like a great opportunity. But it wasn't a good match for anyone else.

David had his, I've had mine and you will have yours. So keep an eye out for your opportunities disguised as challenges and be forever ready to seize them.

As the famous Latin phrase *"carpe diem"* implores us to do, we should seize the day and make the most of every opportunity – and challenge!

Now let's take our final few steps together, on the next page.

CHAPTER TWENTY-FOUR:

YOUR 7 KEYS QUESTIONNAIRE

So here we are. Just one more test of your reading comprehension before you enjoy the dramatic grand finale Epilogue that follows this review.

Here again you have multiple-choice questions and another optional essay question. Let's see what you know about these keys!

1. Your birthplace or hometown can:

    A. Help shape your sense of identity

    B. Position you strategically in some way

    C. Either limit or expand your opportunities

    D. Be a positive or negative springboard

    E. All of the above

2. Your family birth order is:

    A. An iron-clad predictor of your comfort and success

    B. One element of your personal makeup

    C. A possible key to your best role or comfort zone

    D. Both B and C

3. Your personality traits are:

    A. Impossible to identify

    B. Always crystal clear

    C. Key factors to finding your best fit and happiness

    D. Important for relating with others and getting along

    E. Both C and D

4. Grit, guts and gumption are:

    A. A natural sugar-free breakfast cereal

    B. A popular barbeque dish in the south

    C. Important traits not found on personality tests

    D. A musical trio from Memphis, Tennessee

5. When it comes to gifts, talents and skills:

    A. You can always buy or borrow other people's gifts

    B. Mozart and Beethoven had mad skills but no special gifts

    C. Charisma is a skill everyone can develop

    D. Most people can develop skills with practice

6. Martin Luther King Jr. and Joan of Arc were:

    A. Driven by inspirational visions and dreams

    B. Killed for pursuing their causes

    C. Able to share their messages in compelling ways

    D. All the above

7. From Walt Disney we learn that:

    A. Vision is our ability to see the future with imagination

    B. His first company failed on his way to success

   C. Mickey Mouse was first named Mortimer

   D. He turned his creative vision into solid plans and products

   E. All the above

8. David's reference to a lion and a bear was:

   A. Evidence of his obsession with stuffed animals

   B. A simple nod to his favorite pets

   C. Sharing his "relatable experience" facing deadly foes

9. Revisiting your victories is important because:

   A. You want to puff yourself up like a big "winner"

   B. You will never feel or dwell on painful defeats

   C. Remembering wins can bolster your confidence

   D. We dwell on losses, so recalling wins can balance that

   E. Both C and D

10. The important thing about recognizing seasons is:

   A. It helps you maintain a big-picture view of life

   B. You know they will usually pass in time

   C. You should dress appropriately

   D. You should make the most out of them

   E. All of the above (Yes, C is no joke!)

11. The brightest "green light" for seizing opportunity is:

   A. A big pile of money

   B. Everyone thinks you should

   C. You can't think of anything else at the moment

   D. It fits you in an extraordinary (and hopefully convergent) way

12. **Essay Question: Which chapter or key is most compelling to you? What story or example in these 7 Key chapters comes to mind or speaks to your situation best? Any other thoughts or reflections on these topics?**

Take a moment to write down your answer, jot down notes or just reflect in your own mind. And feel free to share your thoughts with me at essays@HitYourBullseye.com.

ANSWER KEY

1. E
2. D
3. E
4. C
5. D
6. D
7. E
8. C
9. E
10. E
11. D
12. Go to essays@hityourbullseye.com if you'd like to share.

Now let's read the dramatic Epilogue and claim our special prize...

YOUR NOBEL PRIZE

There once was a man named Alfred. He was a Swedish chemist and engineer who invented dynamite, back in the 1800s.

Alfred and his family became very wealthy over the years thanks to their involvement in land development, mining, construction and military products.

One day in 1888 he opened the newspaper and read his own obituary – and was understandably shocked!

Apparently, several papers had confused the death of his brother Ludwig with his own passing. Such an accident was painful and unfortunate, to say the least.

But what really hurt Alfred was the paper's brutal characterization of his life as presented under the banner headline, "The Merchant of Death is Dead."

The story branded him as a bloodthirsty war-baron, bombmaker and arms profiteer rather than a brilliant and peace-loving man of progress and public welfare.

Alfred's last name was Nobel. And his name seemed to mean all the wrong things. So naturally he was grieved.

Nobel's grief turned to inspiration, however, when he thought about creating a legacy of peace and progress for humanity, somehow associated with his name.

Alfred Nobel decided to rewrite his will and leave all his assets to establish an endowment to fund annual "Nobel prizes" to recognize and reward outstanding people around the world who make exceptional contributions to humanity.

These prizes were to be given in the fields of science, medicine, economics, literature and peace, with the first ones awarded in 1901.

The Nobel Prize has endured ever since; currently, over $1 million is granted to each award winner.

THE ULTIMATE PRIZE

When promoting my book or otherwise sharing the "bullseye" message of personal convergence, I often say, "It's never too early or too late to live on-target."

And Alfred Nobel's story colorfully illustrates that truth for us.

Any day short of the grave grants us new and wonderful opportunities to make a positive difference, to achieve and share success and to enjoy the journey.

Nobel's story illuminates even more.

We all know the Ebenezer Scrooge type of story (in Charles Dickens' *A Christmas Carol*) that unfolds just before the finish line. But for most of us, the process of targeting and directing our lives is far less theatrical and can start much earlier.

We may not pull a complete 180 turnaround on Christmas Eve or win, fund or bestow any world-renowned gifts or prizes. (Though we can certainly aspire to do so.)

The truth is that we have already won Nobel's greatest prize.

That prize is the timeless perspective his life story offers us. His story encourages us to look not only toward our ultimate destiny, but all the way back from that end point, to consider our life's overarching message.

What will it be?

Positive impact? Shared success? Generosity? Happiness and joy?

This is what it means to "start with the end in mind," and to even think about our own obituaries, and what they might say or convey.

Some suggest we even write highlights of who we are or have been, and who we want to become today, tomorrow and in the days ahead.

Feel free to share yours at essays@hityourbullseye.com, and be blessed as you harness and direct all your greatest experiences, dreams and attributes toward an epic life of impact, success and happiness – and toward your ultimate destiny.

Let's go!

WHAT NOW? WHAT NEXT?

If you would like a free "Next Steps" worksheet,
simply request it at hello@hityourbullseye.com.
You can also get a free 7 Keys Summary
at hityourbullseye.com/free.

MY HUMBLE REQUEST:

As you know, positive Reviews, Likes
and Follows are very important these days.
If you've enjoyed this book, would you
mind clicking those buttons and sharing your
thoughts on Amazon, Instagram or elsewhere,
while it's still fresh in your mind?
Thank you so much!

Made in the USA
Columbia, SC
09 March 2024

32366391R10098